Keeping up with the Times

Keeping up with the Times

Diversity and Inclusion in Early Childhood Teacher Education Programs

Edited by
Mari Riojas-Cortez

ROWMAN & LITTLEFIELD
Lanham • Boulder • New York • London

Published by Rowman & Littlefield
An imprint of The Rowman & Littlefield Publishing Group, Inc.
4501 Forbes Boulevard, Suite 200, Lanham, Maryland 20706
www.rowman.com

6 Tinworth Street, London SE11 5AL, United Kingdom

Copyright © 2021 by Mari Riojas-Cortez

All rights reserved. No part of this book may be reproduced in any form or by any electronic or mechanical means, including information storage and retrieval systems, without written permission from the publisher, except by a reviewer who may quote passages in a review.

British Library Cataloguing in Publication Information Available

Library of Congress Cataloging-in-Publication Data

Names: Riojas-Cortez, Mari, editor.
Title: Keeping up with the times : diversity and inclusion in early childhood teacher education programs / Edited by Mari Riojas-Cortez.
Description: Lanham : Rowman & Littlefield, [2021] | Includes bibliographical references. | Summary: "In this book the contributors reflect on the issues they have encountered in their programs related to diversity."—Provided by publisher.
Identifiers: LCCN 2021000801 (print) | LCCN 2021000802 (ebook) | ISBN 9781475853582 (cloth) | ISBN 9781475853599 (paperback) | ISBN 9781475853605 (epub)
Subjects: LCSH: Early childhood teachers—Training of. | Early childhood teachers—In-service training. | Inclusive education. | Multicultural education. | Educational equalization.
Classification: LCC LB1775.6 .K44 2021 (print) | LCC LB1775.6 (ebook) | DDC 372.21—dc23
LC record available at https://lccn.loc.gov/2021000801
LC ebook record available at https://lccn.loc.gov/2021000802

To all early childhood teacher educators and their students.

Contents

Foreword ix
Bekisizwe S. Ndimande

Preface xiii

Introduction xv
Mari Riojas-Cortez

1 Preparing Early Childhood Teachers for the Importance of
   Seeing Color in Children: Bloom's Taxonomy as a Guide 1
   Kimberly Davidson, Flora Farago, and Terry Husband

2 Addressing lgbtq+ Issues With Preservice Teachers in
   Conservative Spaces 23
   Kenya E. Wolff and Janice Kroeger

3 Ready for Our Immigrant Children: Preparing Early Childhood
   Educators to Work With Immigrant Children and Their Families 45
   Wilma Robles-Meléndez

4 Religion in Early Childhood: Guidelines for Preservice Teachers 61
   *Ruth Vilà-Baños, Montserrat Freixa Niella, Assumpta Aneas
   Alvarez, and Angelina Sánchez Martí*

About the Editor and Contributors 87

Foreword

Bekisizwe S. Ndimande

One of the biggest challenges of the 21st century are the increasing social inequities largely caused by racism, sexism, heterosexism, classism, and cultural and religious intolerance, including the "otherization" of immigrant populations around the world. Yet, some pundits have referred to the United States as "post-racial" since the election of Barack Obama, the 44th U.S. president. All these challenges occur within a sociopolitical and economic environment that harshly marginalizes the minoritized communities in our social institutions, including their children in schools.

Keeping Up with the Times: Diversity and Inclusion in Early Childhood Education Programs couldn't have been published at a better time. Collectively, these chapters raise critical questions about the current state of diversity and inclusion in early childhood programs, not just in the United States, but in other countries as well. By focusing on the intersectionality of race, religion, sexuality, and nationality, the authors collectively ask crucial questions about the effectiveness of programs in preparing teachers for inclusion and diversity in content and pedagogy.

This volume pushes us to think deeply and seriously about the future of our children and their educational opportunities. The argument is clear. If educators and all those involved in the education of our children want to afford all children equal educational opportunities, then discussions of race and racism, sexuality, the politics of religion, and nationality should be at the center of educational reforms.

Understanding that race in the United States was historically institutionalized with the purpose of maintaining white privilege and status quo between white communities and those of color is the first step in striving for inclusion and diversity in early childhood preparation programs. To be silent around issues of race and racism is not a good thing. I have heard some people say:

"Oh, I do not see color in people; I just see human beings." As flattering as these words might sound on the surface, the subtext—whether conscious or unconscious—is that the speaker does not want to acknowledge the history of racial discrimination in this country. It is a history that brings discomfort and guilt to many people.

In reality, racism did not end with the civil rights movement of the 1960s, nor did it end with the election of President Obama. I agree with the authors in this volume who argue that being colorblind is not helpful in teacher education. I would argue that this could also be associated with the concept of the American Dream, a myth purporting that if people work hard enough, they will be rewarded accordingly, as if all people exist on a level playing field, regardless of race. Thus, this volume is a call not just to early childhood teachers, but to all those involved in educating our children, to rethink the construction of race and racism in the United States and how this affects education.

Dispelling the popular belief that young children do not understand race, Chapter 1 provides current research, beyond the groundbreaking experiment by Clark and Clark in 1939, to show that children do indeed understand and are aware of racial difference. Young children do not live in a sociopolitical vacuum. They listen to conversations at kitchen tables, in communities, and are not immune from the mainstream media and internet images about race. They receive explicit and implicit messages about race and racial difference, thus forming their own opinions about racial identities, often based on how they witness people of certain races being spoken about and treated.

Consider an example from Van Ausdale and Feagin's (1996) study involving a 4-year-old white and a 3-year-old Asian American child. The white child was heard telling the Asian American child that she was not supposed to pull a wagon because "Only white Americans can pull this wagon." This volume is consistent with examples from such studies, affirming that 3- to 4-year-old children understand the power of race and can invoke such understanding on the playground. As one of the essays in this volume eloquently argues, early childhood teachers who refuse to discuss race and racism with young children, or who see themselves as colorblind, do children more harm than good. In fact, such a teacher is not helping children to reject racism in spaces where they may encounter it.

The 21st century has also witnessed the rise of heterosexism the attacks on lgbtq+ (lesbian, gay, bisexual, transgender, queer/questioning, and others) communities. While some progress has been made to recognize same-sex marriages, we also witness pushback from different states. This is reminiscent of the suppression of interracial marriages in the United States under Jim Crow laws and in other countries with deep racial divisions such as South Africa under apartheid. Chapter 2 eloquently outlines strategies that can help teachers learn about ways they can engage with and learn from lgbtq+ parents and children.

The chapter also points out larger problems that may result from teacher preparation programs' inadequate engagement with critical sociopolitical ideas and insufficient understanding of the significance of coexistence in a democracy. Like race, young children are aware of existing oppressions, such as bullying in school, that their friends who identify as lgbtq+ and/or who come from lgbtq+ families face. Teaching for inclusion and diversity in early childhood requires teachers who understand that traditional families carry their own hegemony that is deeply entrenched in patriarchal hierarchy, suppressing women and children. Traditional families also operate within the racialized discourse that promotes "blood ties" in order to avoid the degeneration of the White race and its privilege. We need curricula that critically examine the implications of traditional families and that promote learning and understanding of lgbtq+ families.

Chapter 3 in this volume also acknowledges that when families and communities migrate across borders, the education of their children is impacted. While a few immigrant families and communities are rewarded with the positive effects of upward social mobility, a large number of children in immigrant families experience negative attitudes and everyday discrimination in educational contexts and beyond. Racism, xenophobia, cultural exclusion, and other forms of discrimination can have a direct devastating impact on the education of immigrant children.

In fact, xenophobia is prevalent outside the United States as well. We hear of incidents of racial discrimination in countries such as South Africa, Italy, Russia, France, and Hungary, to mention but a few. In the United States, border control has become increasingly aggressive toward Mexican and Latin American immigrants. Take, for instance, those immigrant children who were protected by DACA (Deferred Action for Childhood Arrivals) which at the time of this writing was on the verge of being rescinded.

Keeping up with the Times: Diversity and Inclusion in Early Childhood Education Programs also raises complicated and complex positions about religion in the education of young children. There is no question that religion has historically been used to Christianize and "civilize" those who were presumed to be "barbaric" and "primitive." The proliferation of missionary schools around the world, including the traumatic efforts that forced Native American children into boarding schools, carry lingering memories of colonialization and the Europeanization of the "Other."

While cognizant of the separation between church and state in the United States, Chapter 4 presents an alternate role for spirituality in the education of young children. In the context of intercultural and interreligious dialogue in education, the work in this book can help us realize that families and communities are diverse, and that diversity in religion and spirituality should be respected rather than curtailed.

As I conclude this foreword, let me first recognize the authors for such an exceptional volume. It offers potential solutions for early childhood and teacher education preparation programs, including Head Start and public schools. It also provides a vivid reminder of the struggles of minoritized communities who have been otherized by some of our social institutions. No matter their social oppression, these communities have formed alliances with progressive educators to continue to be resilient and push back in an effort to fight for inclusive and equitable education for all children. I am certain the readers will agree that this volume brings a glimmer of hope to the next generation of early childhood educators.

REFERENCES

Clark, K. B., & Clark, M. K. (1939). The development of consciousness of self and the emergence of racial identification in Negro preschool children. *Journal of Social Psychology, 10*(4), 591–599. doi:10.1080/00224545.1939.9713394

Van Ausdale, D., & Feagin, J. R. (1996). Using racial and ethnic concepts: The critical case of very young children. *American Sociological Review, 61*(5), 779–793.

Preface

The idea for a book about how institutions of higher education (IHEs) are keeping up with diversity was derived from a roundtable conference presentation. A group of early childhood faculty had been discussing major issues that they face in their programs as they tried to emphasize different topics within diversity. After the positive feedback from the presentation, we decided to expand the topics and share it with a greater audience by developing an edited book that discussed ideas and concepts centered around diversity that we, as early childhood faculty, knew that preservice teachers needed to know.

The responsibility for creating a qualified teaching workforce rests with many but, most importantly, with institutions of higher education. As such, it is an IHE's responsibility to work with future and current early childhood educators in order to prepare them to provide high-quality experiences to children and families. Given the complex nature of diversity, it is just as important for faculty to be prepared to integrate such topics within courses, particularly in early childhood education courses.

Diversity first must be defined within different contexts and groups. Given the recent changes in the demographics and views on social issues in the United States, we critically analyze if or how early childhood teacher preparation programs have kept up with current themes and topics that impact children and families, including understanding the issue of race in early childhood and the reluctance of some early childhood educators to discuss it with young children; the misconceptions about lgbtq+ students and families; the importance of the complexities of immigrant families, and understanding diversity within the context of religious beliefs.

The realities of diversity in our society are one of the elements demanding attention in early childhood teacher preparation as we help create teachers who, in turn, will help create high-quality early childhood programs. The main objective and unique feature of this book are the IHE program samples that give information regarding diversity that would be useful and beneficial for preservice teachers. The information also provides opportunities for in-depth analysis of preservice teachers' beliefs regarding diverse populations.

Introduction

Mari Riojas-Cortez

Preparation for early childhood teachers occurs in different ways. If preservice teachers are seeking teacher certification or licensure to teach in the public schools, they can go through an institution of higher education (IHE) or through alternative ways of getting certified, such as programs provided by state agencies. Not all early childhood teacher preparation programs are the same, but they should offer courses that may help preservice teachers become knowledgeable about diverse children and their families.

Effective early childhood teacher preparation programs must provide courses and professional experiences that focus on child development, but from a diverse perspective. In addition, play, dual language development, early (bi)literacy development, partnerships with parents, socioemotional development, and pedagogical knowledge should all be included as part of the program. The courses should guide the preservice teachers to develop knowledge and skills that will help them become well prepared to work with young children and their families, particularly the children and families of diverse backgrounds.

However, taking courses is no guarantee that preservice teachers would effectively work with diverse young children and families, as we all have different beliefs and dispositions. Nevertheless, principles of social justice must be the foundation of university or professional development programs in order to better prepare preservice teachers to work with diverse families. A strong vision is needed in order to create such programs; in essence, faculty must examine their own bias as well (Colbert, 2010).

Indeed, there is a dire need for reform in early childhood teacher preparation programs to include "multicultural/intercultural issues" (Palaiologou & Dimitriadou, 2013, p. 49). We agree that a reform is imperative, but we cannot reform what we don't know or understand. As IHE educators, we must be prepared to understand that preservice teachers already come to us with "beliefs about children, classroom practice, and guidance of children's behavior" (Di Santo, Timmons, & Lenis, 2017, p. 223). Such beliefs are often difficult to change.

The challenge with having predetermined beliefs about diverse children and families is that teacher beliefs very often do not match those of the children they teach. This can also happen in the higher education classroom. Often IHE faculty have predetermined beliefs, and if their beliefs and dispositions toward diverse children and families show bias, then it is likely those beliefs will be shared by preservice teachers. The chapters in this book help us explore difficult topics.

An important topic to understand, and one that is often not included, is the diversity of religions. For instance, in the majority of the southern United States, Christianity is the practiced religion. The Pew Research Center shows that 70% of families in the U.S. South comprise a variety of "Christian faiths," while 5.9% practice non-Christian faiths. Preservice teachers' religious beliefs are often in dissonance with those of diverse families. Some studies have shown that previous experience with cultural and religious diversity provides a more positive attitude toward children and families of diverse religious beliefs (Vilá, Rubio, & Aneas, 2018).

Furthermore, attitudes toward diverse families, including those having different structures and identifying as lgbtq+ (lesbian, gay, bisexual, transgender, queer/questioning, and other), may hinder the relationship between parent and teacher, resulting in undesirable experiences for the young child. We can see the differences particularly when students come from homes with conservative religious beliefs. Similarly, our political beliefs or attitudes toward difficult topics such as immigration may hinder perceptions of children, particularly dual-language learners in the schools (Kolano & King, 2015) who are often labeled "at-risk" and are seen through a deficit lens.

D'Haem and Griswold (2017) found that student teachers are often "unaware" of the importance of working with diverse families, and view any problems encountered as "attributable to the parents" (p. 81). Lack of awareness and negative attitudes form part of personal views that unfortunately permeate teaching practices when early childhood teacher preparation programs do not adequately prepare preservice teachers. This is part of the deficit discourse experienced by children of color, who are often marginalized not only by preservice teachers, but by university faculty who may be biased regarding a particular group or groups.

Diversity within classrooms is very real in communities across the globe (Hinojosa Pareja & López López, 2018) and the United States (Taylor, Kumi-Yeboah, & Ringlaben, 2016). Because preservice teachers will be working with children, it is important to analyze and discuss their beliefs regarding diverse children, as those beliefs can greatly affect classroom practices. We agree that it is imperative that public schools institute the importance of "acceptance, respect, and inclusion" (Sanders, Haselden, & Moss, 2013, p. 171). However, when some children have to be "included," the message is that they don't belong.

Chiner, Cardona-Moltó, and Gómez Puerta (2015) note that there are two ways that teachers see diversity: from a personal and from a professional perspective. The personal perspective includes opinions, expectations, and judgements housed within the teacher's personal context. The professional view may involve educational issues such as instructional practices or resources. Some preservice teachers have positive dispositions regarding diverse backgrounds, and others do not.

Consider the following excerpt from one undergraduate student at a Hispanic-serving institution. The student was participating in a family early literacy program for families and young children. The student's major concern was not being prepared; she felt frustrated, but as she began to interact and work with the parents (who were immigrants from different countries), she changed her disposition:

> After talking to these parents and getting to know a bit of their history, I felt all of my frustration leave me. The biggest thing I felt was compassion, and I saw a drive in these families that is unparalleled to anything I have ever seen. The fact that they were from different cultures and spoke different languages was not stopping them from pursuing a happy life with their family. It made me realize just how important it is to take a step back, and appreciate all cultures and backgrounds, because everyone has their own unique story.

This excerpt shows us how this student feels about immigrant families. Her disposition is a positive one in that she is focusing on how immigrant parents want to pursue a happy life with their families.

Culture and ethnicity are two very important aspects of diversity. Another aspect is income, and some preservice teachers may feel apprehensive when working with families having different economic backgrounds, as indicated by one of the students participating in the same project:

> How can I connect with these parents and children from lower-income households? I fear that I will not know how to connect with these parents and children because I do not come from a lower-income household. I hope that I will be able to build a good relationship with them, regardless.

This student's disposition is also a positive one. Although he does not share the same socioeconomic background with these families, he wants to develop a good relationship with them. Unfortunately, not all students share positive dispositions; some have negative views of parents in different areas of diversity.

Many preservice teachers come to teacher preparation programs with biases and prejudices that may be somewhat difficult to change. I recall one student, also participating in the same family literacy program, who said that the parents she was working with only went to the program because they wanted to get the free gift card, but didn't really care for their children. Such negative perceptions of childrens' parents often hinder learning and teaching opportunities and, as such, affect the school experience.

DIVERSITY IN EARLY CHILDHOOD

How do we begin to understand diversity in early childhood in order to combat biases? There are many layers of diversity within families that are important to examine. We must consider ethnic diversity first and foremost as we engage in a conversation regarding diversity, as we know (or should know) the history of people of color in the United States and the challenges and adversities they have experienced. In the context of this book, understanding diversity begins with a definition that encompasses the realities of many families across the United States.

We agree with Loveridge et al. (2012), who regard diversity as "differences of social significance among people based on dimensions such as class, ethnicity, gender, sexual orientation, dis/abilities, languages, special learning needs, family formation, health, religion, and citizenship status" (p. 102). We also see the importance of talking about race within the context of early childhood.

Loveridge et al. (2012) indicate that context is very important when discussing diversity. The context of diversity also includes historical aspects, particularly for groups that often have been marginalized such as Latinos and African Americans in the United States. For young children of color, the marginalization occurs in different ways, but particularly through adult biases toward them that affect the way these adults teach and assess what the children know.

Currently we see immigrant children and families being marginalized by penalizing them through separation (Cervantes, Ullrich, & Matthews, 2018) and African American families living in fear for their safety (Treva, 2018). Families in poverty may feel threatened by changes in policies that would result in even more drastic impacts on their lives, and families of different structures may face discrimination for having a different lifestyle (Church et al., 2018). Regardless of an educator's political stance, children and families must be respected and treated with dignity.

PRESERVICE EARLY CHILDHOOD TEACHERS: PREPARED FOR DIVERSITY?

Institutions of higher education are responsible for working with future early childhood teachers so that once they begin their teaching careers, they are not only knowledgeable regarding diversity, but also know how to create contexts that meet the needs of diverse learners. Some teacher preparation programs in IHEs offer courses that focus on multicultural education (Sleeter, 2001). However, unless diversity is built into the foundation of the program, preservice teachers will not be prepared for diversity. This is not keeping up with the times.

The current state of affairs tells us that there is a high need for early childhood educators who are prepared to work with diverse populations. Given the recent changes in the demographics (Flores, 2017) and views on social issues in the United States, we must critically analyze how early teacher preparation programs have kept up with current changes, including addressing preservice teachers' beliefs and dispositions regarding issues of race and color, sexual orientation and lgbtq+ families, the complexities of immigrant families, and the role of religion.

The reality of diversity in our society is just one of the elements demanding attention in early childhood teacher preparation. Awareness of the implications of diversity in achieving quality in early education practices requires continual, intentional efforts (Derman-Sparks, 2009). For example, understanding the complexities of immigrant families (particularly those who are not documented) is crucial for early childhood teachers, but how well early childhood teachers are prepared to work with these families is unknown (Goodwin, 2017).

The authors of this book reflect on the issues related to diversity that they have encountered in their programs. This reflection helps us understand the importance of being prepared and having an open disposition toward diversity. It is our hope that you continue to share ideas as we continue on the journey of diversity and work to keep up with the times.

REFERENCES

Cervantes, W., Ullrich, R., & Matthews, H. (2018). *Our children's fear: Immigration policy's effects on young children*. Center for Law and Social Policy, Inc. (CLASP). https://www.clasp.org/sites/default/files/publications/2018/03/2018_ourchildrensfears.pdf

Chiner, E., Cardona-Moltó, M., & Gómez-Puerta, J. M. (2015). Teachers' beliefs about diversity: An analysis from a personal and professional perspective. *New Approaches in Educational Research, 4*(1), 18–23.

Church, J., Hegde, A. V., Averett, P., & Ballard, S. M. (2018). Early childhood administrators' attitudes and experiences in working with gay- and lesbian-parented families. *Early Child Development and Care, 188*(2), 264–280.

Colbert, P. J. (2010). Developing a culturally responsive classroom collaborative of faculty, students, and institution. *Contemporary Issues in Education Research, 3*(9), 17–26.

Derman-Sparks, L. (2009) Children-socioeconomic class and equity. *Young Children, 64*(3), 50–53.

D'Haem, J., & Griswold, P. (2017). Teacher educators' and student teachers' beliefs about preparation for working with families including those from diverse socioeconomic backgrounds. *Education and Urban Society, 49*(1), 81–109.

Di Santo, A., Timmons, K., & Lenis, A. (2017). Pre-service early childhood educators' pedagogical beliefs. *Journal of Early Childhood Teacher Education, 88*(3), 223–241.

Flores, A. (2017). How the U.S. Hispanic population is changing: Fact Tank. Pew Research Center. http://www.pewresearch.org/fact-tank/2017/09/18/how-the-u-s-hispanic-population-is-changing/

Goodwin, L. (2017). Who is in the classroom now? Teacher preparation and the education of immigrant children. *Educational Studies, 53*(5), 433–449.

Hinojosa Pareja, E. F., & López López, M. C. (2018). Interculturality and teacher education: A study from preservice teachers' perspective. *Australian Journal of Teacher Education, 43*(3), 74–92.

Palaiologou, N., & Dimitriadou, C. (2013). Multicultural/intercultural education issues in pre-service teacher education courses: The case of Greece. *Multicultural Education Review, 5*(2), 49–84.

Kolano, L. Q., & King, E. T. (2015). Preservice teachers' perceived beliefs towards English language learners: Can a single course change attitudes? *Issues in Teacher Education, 24*(2), 3–21.

Loveridge, J., Rosewarne, S., Shuker, M. J., Barker, A., & Nager, J. (2012). Responding to diversity: Statements and practices in two early childhood education contexts. *European Early Childhood Education Research Journal, 20*(1), 99–113.

Sanders, M. S., Haselden, K., & Moss, R. M. (2013). Teaching diversity to preservice teachers: Encouraging self-reflection and awareness to develop successful teaching practices. *Multicultural Learning and Teaching, 9*(2), 171–185.

Sleeter, C. E. (2001). Preparing teachers for culturally diverse schools: Research and the overwhelming presence of whiteness. *Journal of Teacher Education, 52*(2), 94–106.

Taylor, R., Kumi-Yeboah, A., & Ringlaben, R. P. (2016). Pre-service teachers' perceptions towards multicultural education and teaching of culturally and linguistically diverse learners. *Multicultural Education, 23*(3–4), 42–48.

Treva, L. B. (2018). Ain't nobody got time for that: Anti-Black girl violence in the era of #SayHerName. *Urban Education, 53*(2), 162–175.

Vilá, R., Rubio, M. J., & Aneas, A. (2018). The attitudes of future educational agents to religious and cultural diversity in education in Catalonia. *Education Reform Journal, 3*(1), 15–23.

Chapter One

Preparing Early Childhood Teachers for the Importance of Seeing Color in Children

Bloom's Taxonomy as a Guide

Kimberly Davidson, Flora Farago, and Terry Husband

Let's debunk the myth that children do not see skin color. Or that anyone does not see racial and color differences. Children and adults *see color* by explicitly noticing differences, but also through implicit awareness of power dynamics associated with social constructions of race. Examples in the literature have shown this to be true, even for children as young as three years of age. Studies have shown that preschool-aged children engage in spontaneous and child-initiated conversations related to race and ethnicity in ways that involve alliances, conflict, and competition (Aukrust & Rydland, 2009; Park, 2011; Van Ausdale & Feagin, 2001).

Learning about and naming colors is a frequent area of inquiry and development for toddlers as they engage in categorization tasks and assimilate new terminologies. Yet, when preschool-age children exhibit a natural curiosity regarding color differences in human skin tones, their inquiries are often dismissed or silenced. Educators in the early childhood field have traditionally been taught that acknowledging color (and indirectly, cultural or racial) differences in the children they teach should be avoided, partially in response to the history of blatant racism in this country.

Although overt racism, such as the use of racial epithets, and segregation were once legal, in the post–civil rights era any discussion of race was seen as taboo. Conversations around race are sometimes regarded as too complex for young children to comprehend. Indoctrinating a colorblind philosophy in early childhood settings—or teaching children not to see skin color and silence their inquiries about race—can negatively impact identity development in children of color and impede understanding and appreciation of racial diversity for all children.

Several scholars have recognized the contradiction of causing harm not by talking about race, but by *not* talking about it, and call on teachers and caregivers to avoid colorblind philosophies in early childhood education programs (e.g., Boutte, Lopez-Robertson, & Powers-Costello, 2011; Farago, Davidson, & Byrd, 2019; Kemple, Lee, & Harris, 2016). Early childhood educators need to guide children's understanding of race, racism, and racial justice as a means of helping them develop a positive racial and ethnic identity, a critical consciousness, and confidence in recognizing, naming, and interrupting racism.

Early childhood teacher preparation programs have a responsibility to guide preservice teachers through processes of confronting their own biases, developing beliefs and skill sets that enable them to *see color* in children and families, and becoming culturally competent leaders who partner with families from diverse backgrounds. Furthermore, professional agencies within the field of early childhood education frequently update standards and learning objectives as the needs of children and families evolve.

For example, the Office of Head Start updated and revised its *Multicultural Principles for Early Childhood Leaders* resource to highlight the important role of culture in children's development and the need for culturally competent early childhood professionals (U.S. Department of Health and Human Services, 2018). Likewise, the National Association for the Education of Young Children (NAEYC) has released a position statement outlining principles of equity in early childhood (2019). Interpreting those standards and applying them to real-world scenarios and classrooms is the important work of teacher preparation programs.

To aid teacher educators and early childhood professionals as they consider the importance of becoming racially competent and race-conscious educators, this chapter utilizes Bloom's Taxonomy as a guide for preparing early childhood teachers to see color—that is, acknowledge race—in the children in their care. Originally published in 1956 as the *Taxonomy of Educational Objectives*, Bloom's Taxonomy is a framework employed by educators for decades in order to understand the learning process.

Bloom and collaborators describe knowledge as the first objective of and a precondition for other cognitive tasks and abilities. Once acquiring knowledge, learners work through a hierarchical process of comprehension, application, analysis, synthesis, and evaluation. Contemporary scholars (Anderson & Krathwohl, 2001) revised the original taxonomy to incorporate action words into descriptions of cognitive processes (table 1.1).

Bloom's Taxonomy is a useful guide for early childhood teacher educators as they examine cultural competency and race-conscious practices within their course content, degree requirements, and pedagogical practices. Utilizing the levels of Bloom's Taxonomy to guide understanding of cognitive processes provides a clear path for mentoring preservice teachers as they begin a lifelong journey of understanding (and ultimately embracing) the roles of race, ethnicity, and culture in their own lives and in the lives of children and families with whom they work.

BUILDING DEVELOPMENTAL KNOWLEDGE OF RACE AND ETHNICITY

The foundational level of Bloom's Taxonomy is *knowledge*. Learners demonstrate knowledge primarily through methods of recall and remembering. Building a base of developmental knowledge of race and ethnicity in early childhood teacher preparation programs requires including the large body of literature on young children's racial awareness and early displays of prejudice.

Racial Awareness and Implicit Bias

Early studies of young children's racial understandings focused on the attitudes and values children attributed to racial categories rather than the development of broader social constructions of race and ethnicity. The well-known doll studies conducted by Clark and Clark (1939) are some of the earliest examples of methods in which children are shown a doll, drawing, or photograph and asked to ascribe meaning to color differences.

At the time, studies were interpreted as evidence of perpetual low self-esteem in children of color, though recent critics have argued against the

Table 1.1. Action Words from the Revised Bloom's Taxonomy

Remember	Understand	Apply	Analyze	Evaluate	Create
Recognizing	Interpreting	Executing	Differentiating	Checking	Generating
Recalling	Exemplifying	Implementing	Organizing	Critiquing	Planning
	Classifying		Attributing		Producing
	Summarizing				
	Inferring				
	Comparing				
	Explaining				

Source: Anderson & Krathwohl (2001).

oversimplification of this interpretation. For example, Trawick-Smith (2018) describes a "myth of self-hatred" in which studies of children's self-esteem led some scholars to conclude that children of color held internal negative views of themselves based solely on skin color.

Early studies have been criticized as a result of more recent findings that doll identification and self-esteem were not related (Byrd, 2012) and that children chose the doll that matched their skin color when the interviewer was of the same cultural background as the child (Annis & Corenblum, 1986). Nevertheless, studies utilized and continued to build on Clark and Clark's initial methods of identifying racial attitudes in young children.

Williams and Roberson (1967) adapted the method to include drawings instead of dolls in the Preschool Racial Attitude Measure (PRAM). Results from their studies were consistent with previous studies in which the majority of children exhibited pro-white/anti-Black biases. Several other studies (e.g., Dunham, Chen, & Banaji, 2013; Hirschfeld, 2008; Patterson & Bigler, 2006) suggest that young children may hold implicit, and in some cases explicit, biases toward various groups of people in society.

Williams and Steele (2019) examined bias in 359 white children measured via three procedures: Affective Priming Task, Affective Misattribution Procedure, and the Implicit Association Test. Findings revealed that 5- to 8-year-old children consistently demonstrated in-group and pro-white favoritism toward the white child exemplars.

Dunham and others (2013) found that children as young as age three began to show implicit racial biases against people from different groups. Their qualitative study included 883 racially and ethnically diverse children aged 3 to 14. Participants viewed a series of faces on a computer screen and categorized each as Black, white, or Asian. Results showed white children categorized the angry faces they saw on the computer screen as Black more often than white. Similarly, Taiwanese children categorized the angry faces as Black more often than the non-angry faces.

Studies such as these collectively demonstrate the potential development of implicit racial biases toward various groups in society from an early age. Most of the aforementioned studies have been conducted in laboratory or artificial settings; however, a limited number of studies conducted in classrooms also underscore that children notice, make judgements about, and do not ignore race (e.g., Beneke & Cheatham, 2019; Van Ausdale & Feagin, 2001).

Ethnic-Racial Socialization

To draw on research conducted in more naturalistic settings with children and families, teacher education programs can turn to the vast body of research on parental ethnic-racial socialization practices. Decades of research with parents of color indicate engagement in ethnic-racial socialization, which entails relaying messages to children about racial or cultural pride, racial identity, racial bias and discrimination, and egalitarianism (Hughes et al., 2006). The extensive benefits of ethnic-racial socialization range from psychosocial and behavioral (Wang, Henry et al., 2020) to academic (Wang, Smith et al. 2020) and identity outcomes (Huguley et al., 2019).

There is great variability among parents of color regarding the extent and nature of their ethnic-racial socialization practices, but as a whole, parents of color engage in far more racial socialization practices than white parents, who tend to avoid and be largely silent around issues of race and racism (Loyd & Gaither, 2018; Pahlke, Bigler, & Suizzo, 2012; Vittrup, 2018; Zucker & Patterson, 2018). Traditionally focused on parents of adolescents, researchers in this area are increasingly finding that parents of color engage in ethnic-racial socialization with children starting in the early childhood years (e.g., Barbarin & Jean-Baptiste, 2013; Blanchard et al., 2019; Caughy, Nettles, & Lima, 2011; Curenton, Crowley, & Mouzon, 2018; Doucet, 2008; Doucet, Banerjee, & Parade, 2018; Lesane-Brown et al., 2010).

Methods of parental racial socialization of young children of color, such as in the case of Black children, include being proactive and intentional about addressing race and culture, celebrating cultural traditions, having positive interactions with role models who are Black, exposing children to people, groups, or environments that defy racial stereotypes, and being surrounded by peers, neighbors, and educators who are Black (Blanchard et al., 2019). Studies of young Black children indicate that mothers of toddlers feel the need for protecting their children from racism and discrimination, and disclosed examples of their children as young as four being victims to racist incidents (Curenton et al., 2018).

For children of color, feeling positive about one's racial and ethnic background can buffer harmful effects of racism and discrimination (Marcelo & Yates, 2019). Literature reviews consistently demonstrate extensive benefits of positive racial identity via a host of outcomes such as socioemotional skills, academic achievement, and resilience (for reviews, see Miller-Cotto & Byrnes, 2016; Rivas-Drake et al., 2014; University of Pittsburgh School of Education, Race and Early Childhood Collaborative, 2016).

Thus, ethnic-racial socialization should not be excluded from educational course content on young children's development. Preservice teachers need to comprehend the important role of positive messages about race in the lives of children of color.

Section Summary

Given evidence of young children's racial awareness, development of racial biases and stereotypes, and positive effects of ethnic-racial socialization, educators preparing early childhood teachers should include these studies in early childhood developmental coursework. As professionals who "recognize that children are best understood and supported in the context of family, culture, community, and society" (NAEYC, 2019, p. 1), it is imperative to build knowledge of developing racial awareness in order to promote positive racial and ethnic identities in young children.

Suggestion for practice: Include children's developing racial awareness, evidence of prejudice development, the role of ethnic-racial socialization, and benefits of positive racial and ethnic identity in the foundational coursework of early childhood teacher preparation programs.

DEVELOPING EMPATHY AND EXAMINING PERSONAL BELIEF SYSTEMS

The second level of Bloom's Taxonomy is *comprehension*. To comprehend is to understand content beyond mere recall, but lacking the foresight of connections between parts or clear understanding of the bigger picture. Comprehension calls for organizing, comparing, and interpreting the information presented (Anderson & Krathwohl, 2001; Bloom, 1956). Building upon knowledge of children's racial awareness and racial and ethnic identity, early childhood teacher preparation courses should guide preservice teachers in comprehending the deeply rooted influence of race and culture in not only the lives of children and families, but also in their own lives.

Much attention has been drawn to the majority white teaching workforce in comparison to the increasingly diverse population of children in the United States, a mismatch that may have a negative impact on school readiness gains and developing social competence (Downer et al., 2016). Recent data from the Early Childhood Workforce Index is promising, showing the teaching workforce in early childhood is not as racially homogenous as K–12 education (Whitebook et al., 2018). In fact, nearly 40% of early childhood educators are persons of color, compared to only 20% of elementary and secondary educators.

This bodes well for the potential of positive ethnic-racial socialization and identity building in early childhood classrooms. Further, listening to the experiences of early childhood educators of color in teacher preparation programs can inform the field, teacher preparation faculty, and institutions about practices that welcome and affirm, rather than alienate or push out, educators of color from the early childhood arena (Souto-Manning & Cheruvu, 2016).

Teachers as Agents of Socialization

Research on ethnic-racial socialization has traditionally been conducted with parents and family members; however, this line of research is beginning to be

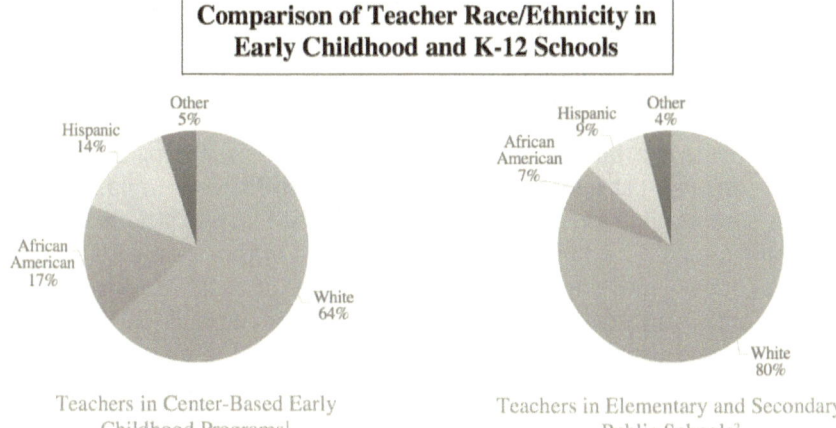

Figure 1.1. A comparison of teacher race/ethnicity in early childhood and K–12 schools. *Source*: Whitebook et al. (2018).

applied to nonfamilial care contexts, including early childhood settings (Aldana & Byrd, 2015; Farago, Davidson, & Byrd, 2019; Farago, Sanders, & Gaias, 2015). Early childhood teachers are in a unique position to shape children's understanding of race.

Outside of the home setting, teachers spend more time with young children than anyone else. Teachers are also considered role models and authority figures by many young children, thus their use of multicultural toys and curricular materials, implicit and explicit interactions with racially diverse children and families, racially disparate discipline practices, and various reactions to children's comments about race and human diversity may have a lasting impact on children in their care.

The current reality is that teachers in general, and early childhood educators in particular, are uncomfortable and unprepared to address race and racism with young children (Boutte et al., 2011; Farago, 2017; Husband, 2012; Vittrup, 2016). Teachers may fear instilling prejudice into children by talking about race and may have (legitimate) concerns about pushback from parents and administrators. However, bravely addressing and confronting issues of race and avoiding colorblind practices is critical for early childhood teachers (Boutte et al., 2011).

It is important for teachers to both listen to children, as well as challenge children, on their ideas around race. Unprepared teachers can potentially traumatize children and alienate parents if they address race in an insensitive or a tokenistic manner. Given research that suggests early childhood educators often feel unprepared to handle discussions of race with young children

(Boutte et al., 2011; Farago, 2017; Husband, 2012; Vittrup, 2016), teacher preparation programs must incorporate self-reflection opportunities followed by competence building exercises.

Whiteness, Privilege, and Colorblindness

Colorblindness is defined as a philosophical and practical approach to teaching and learning that intentionally ignores racial differences in and among various student populations. Many early childhood teachers who believe in and apply a colorblind approach to race in their classrooms argue that children lack the cognitive ability to understand issues of racial marginalization and privilege in meaningful and substantive ways (Boutte et al., 2011). Other early childhood teachers believe that it is controversial to discuss race and racism, and that these conversations should be postponed to later years (Ramsey, 2004).

Early childhood teachers may assume that colorblind approaches will help children develop a positive and healthy appreciation for different racial groups and will ultimately lead children toward identifying and resisting racially injustice acts in society. However, research suggests that choosing not to discuss issues of race and racism with young children makes it difficult for these children to clearly identify and interrupt racism (e.g., Apfelbaum et al., 2010; Boutte et al., 2011).

For early childhood educators who are white, one aspect of reflecting on and examining personal biases entails being cognizant of how colorblindness and white privilege shape identity and teaching practices. Peggy McIntosh (1989) in her seminal piece, "White Privilege: Unpacking the Invisible Knapsack," explains that white privilege confers a set of unearned and unfair advantages on white people. Part of this means that white teachers and parents are not burdened with having to educate children in their care about racism, and they can also be sure that curricular and classroom materials reflect and affirm their and their children's race.

It is critical that white educators acknowledge white privilege and reflect on how whiteness may impact their interactions with families and children of color, their decisions in the classroom, and their teaching in general. As McIntosh proclaims, "teachers must understand where their students 'come from,' and where they themselves come from" (2012, p. 200).

Critical Race Theory (CRT) may be used as a tool to deconstruct whiteness, colorblindness, and racism in education, including in early childhood education contexts (Blaisdell, 2005; Brown, Souto-Manning, & Tropp Laman, 2010; Ladson-Billings, 1998; Summer, 2014). CRT can expose the effects of racism, white supremacy, and white privilege on people. Colorblind ideology and whiteness go hand in hand.

Teachers may acknowledge race in the children they work with, but rarely do they see how whiteness affects their own identities and teaching. Or, teachers may acknowledge white privilege but fail to see how this affects them as teachers. Using the framework of CRT to name whiteness in pedagogical practices, including in disciplinary decisions, may assist teachers with awareness of white privilege (Blaisdell, 2005).

Summer (2014) describes the experience of a "racialized awakening" by a white kindergarten teacher after being called a racist by a Black parent. Summer took this comment as a call for self-reflection and action to name whiteness, to own white privilege, and to commit to a lifetime of anti-oppressive and anti-racist education. Several books and articles are outlined in Summer's piece, which assisted in the author's "racialized awakening" or what some would call "becoming woke." Summer (2014) encourages teachers to question the status quo, often steeped in white, middle-class norms, and to ask questions such as "Who is affirmed and who is left out? Do the hiring patterns reflect the student demographics—why or why not? Who holds the power?" (p. 198).

Other self-reflective questions that teachers can ask themselves include:

> How does my race influence my work as a teacher with my students, especially my students of color? As a teacher, what is the effect of race on my thinking, beliefs, actions, and decision making? How do I, as a teacher, situate myself in the education of others, and how do I negotiate the power structure in my class to allow students to feel a sense of worth regardless of their racial background? How do I situate and negotiate students' knowledge, experiences, expertise, and race with my own? (Milner, 2012, p. 873)

Teachers also need to reflect on their "deficit perspectives" about children of color and their families. This will help to appreciate and value the strengths and resources all families and children bring to school (Doucet, 2008).

Section Summary

Teacher preparation programs have an integral role in preparing early childhood educators who *see color* in children, and celebrate as well as challenge all that comes with acknowledging the role of race in one's life and the lives of others. Teacher preparation programs can use literature on the experiences of teachers of color, and Critical Race Theory as well as literature on white privilege, to encourage preservice teachers to examine and interrogate their beliefs and practices surrounding race. Guided opportunities to critically reflect on one's beliefs and biases will encourage deeper understanding and comprehension of the importance of race in the developmental experiences of children.

Suggestion for practice: Incorporate learning opportunities in mid-level coursework for preservice teachers to demonstrate their understanding of the role that race plays in the lives of children. Learning opportunities should include examining personal belief systems/biases and developing empathy for the experiences of others.

APPLYING PARADIGMS TO PEDAGOGICAL PRACTICES

The third level of Bloom's Taxonomy is *application*. Application of previous knowledge often involves problem solving and putting beliefs into practice. After ensuring early childhood educators have a thorough knowledge of children's developing racial awareness and identity, as well as an understanding of and an ability to critically reflect on their own belief systems and biases, teacher education programs are faced with the challenge of guiding preservice teachers as they apply knowledge and understanding to their pedagogical practices. The challenge arises as a result of myriad curricular and theoretical paradigms seeking to address the multicultural nature of education.

In 1999, Rebecca Bigler published an influential review of multicultural curricula and materials arguing that multicultural programs were ineffective in reducing children's racial and ethnic stereotyping. The author's recommendations included combining strategies based on several theoretical models and calling for effective programs across all levels of schooling (including preschool). Three examples of approaches especially appropriate for early childhood education are presented here. Although not meant to be exhaustive, these brief summaries of each approach are followed by a discussion of their applicability to early childhood education programs (see table 1.2 for a quick reference guide).

Antibias Education

Antibias education is an early childhood framework that encourages educators to bravely address issues of social justice, such as racism, with young children (Derman-Sparks & Edwards, 2010). According to antibias approaches, educators and children should proactively challenge injustices. Educators are encouraged to intentionally address issues of prejudice, stereotyping, and oppression with children, while also celebrating and affirming children's diverse identities.

The antibias education framework includes four goals for children:

1. Demonstrate self-awareness, confidence, family pride, and positive social identities;

Table 1.2. Quick Reference Guide for Racial Paradigms

	Major Components
Antibias Education	(1) self-awareness, confidence, family pride, and positive social identities (2) expression of comfort and joy with human diversity; accurate language for human differences; deep, caring human connections (3) recognition of unfairness, language to describe unfairness, and understanding that unfairness hurts (4) empowerment and the skills to act, with others or alone, against prejudice and/or discriminatory actions
Critical Literacy	(1) disrupting the commonplace (2) interrogating multiple viewpoints (3) focusing on sociopolitical issues (4) promoting social justice
Culturally Responsive Teaching	(1) student learning (academic success) (2) cultural competency (3) sociopolitical consciousness

2. Express comfort and joy with human diversity, accurate language for human differences, and deep, caring human connections;
3. Increasingly recognize unfairness, have language to describe unfairness, and understand that unfairness hurts; and
4. Demonstrate empowerment and the skills to act, with others or alone, against prejudice and/or discriminatory actions. (Derman-Sparks & Edwards, 2010)

Research shows that many early childhood educators are either unfamiliar with antibias approaches, and even those who are familiar with them will find these approaches challenging to implement (Bullock, 1996; Farago, 2017; Van Ausdale & Feagin, 2001). Teachers may silence children, tokenize them, or avoid or change the subject of race. If educators are to be proactive and broach sensitive issues with children, they have to feel prepared and possess the skills to facilitate difficult conversations in ways that cause no harm. Thus, teacher preparation programs have a vital role to play in exposing teachers to antibias curricular approaches and empowering future educators with skills to implement antibias principles with dignity and care.

Critical Literacy

Studies demonstrate that teachers often silence children or fail to engage children in in-depth discussions around race during literacy activities, sometimes dominating the conversation and limiting children's opportunities to share their lived experiences and opinions (Beneke & Cheatham, 2019). Additionally, many of the texts used in early education minimize and marginalize the voices and perspectives of people of color (Derman-Sparks, Ramsey, & Edwards, 2011).

Because early childhood teachers use books that neglect the voices, experiences, and contributions of people of color in their classrooms, young children often develop a view that white people and whiteness are superior to the views and ideologies of people of color in society (Aronson, Callahan, & O'Brien, 2018). Even more important, the lack of exposure to—or, indeed, the sheer absence of—positive images and knowledge related to people of color can lead children to construct negative and stereotypical views about such people.

Taking a critical literacy approach in early childhood classrooms can combat such stereotypical views. A critical literacy approach to education invites early childhood teachers and children to use texts to identify, interrogate, resist, and respond to issues of injustice in humanizing ways. While there are multiple conceptions, theories, and iterations of critical literacy within broader educational scholarship, Lewison, Flint, and Van Sluys's (2002) model of critical literacy is presented here. This model includes four key dimensions of critical literacy: (1) disrupting the commonplace, (2) interrogating multiple viewpoints, (3) focusing on sociopolitical issues, and (4) promoting social justice.

The first dimension, disrupting the commonplace, concerns using language to question the status quo while simultaneously integrating various forms of critical and popular media in the curriculum. An early childhood teacher who is attending to this dimension might purposefully engage students in historical content and concepts that are typically avoided or considered "too controversial" to discuss with young children.

The second dimension deals with interrogating multiple viewpoints. The voices, histories, and perspectives of people of color, women, and other historically marginalized groups are often missing and are silenced in many of the texts used in schools. For this reason, this dimension of critical literacy seeks to highlight, reveal, and center the voices, histories, and perspectives of these groups. An early childhood teacher attending to this dimension might take extra steps to read and incorporate texts that share the narratives of historically marginalized people and groups from firsthand perspectives.

The third dimension deals with sociopolitical aspects of curricula. In clearer terms, early childhood teachers strive to find ways to make connections between what is taught and the various forms of social injustice within the everyday lives of children. For example, given much of the sociopolitical tension surrounding immigration in the United States today, an early childhood teacher who is attending to this particular dimension might purposely read texts and integrate learning activities that humanize people who have migrated from other countries. Ultimately, the goal here is learning to move beyond the acquisition of facts and skills to help children develop a deeper and more critical consciousness of the ways in which the concepts, ideas, and knowledge learned in classrooms connect to broader society.

The fourth dimension of this model concerns promoting social justice. Long-term and sustained change within society cannot occur by simply identifying and discussing issues of injustice in classrooms and schools. Consequently, this fourth dimension of critical literacy encourages early childhood teachers to design and implement actions to resist and combat social injustice in very real and practical ways. For example, an early childhood teacher who is attending to this dimension might, as a group, talk about and write a letter to the president of the United States. A letter could serve as a small, yet powerful and developmentally appropriate, example of how children might assume social action toward combating racism within the larger U.S. society.

Culturally Responsive Teaching

Howard (2018) suggests, "Early childhood educators must recognize that all children come to school with culturally rooted knowledge and with dynamic and complex ways of communicating and learning. When each child's cultural capital is understood, learning can be enhanced by instruction that honors these cultural practices and respectfully teaches new practices rooted in other cultures" (p. 33).

Culturally responsive teaching requires knowing oneself and one's students in such a way that beliefs and values become a part of the classroom learning environment. In a recent interview, Ladson-Billings (2019) reiterated that culturally responsive teaching is not a packaged product, but rather a philosophical approach to teaching. The tenets of culturally responsive teaching have mostly been applied to K–12 education, but are certainly applicable to prekindergarten programs.

The three main areas include student learning (academic success), cultural competency, and sociopolitical consciousness. Perhaps most relevant to early childhood is the underlying premise that conversations, lessons, and topics be generated from student interest. In culturally relevant classrooms, children from diverse backgrounds are valued, engaged, and successful in their learning endeavors. Early childhood teachers who embrace culturally relevant pedagogies go beyond "learning cultures" to develop a deep understanding of children's home experiences and language (Durden, Escalante, & Blitch, 2015).

Recent analyses of data from a 2014 Head Start Family and Child Experiences Survey show discrepancies between parent and staff reports of how families' culture and values are considered when providing services. While 90% of family services staff reported they take parents' culture and values into account *very often*, only 54% of parents felt the same. Additionally, staff reported knowing the background information of families about parental employment and living arrangements, but also reported knowing less about the families' cultural backgrounds and values (Aikens et al., 2017). It is evident that early childhood professionals need to spend time getting to know the families they work with, gaining genuine knowledge of their cultural beliefs, behaviors, traditions, and values that include such components as parenting styles, types of play, and language acquisition.

As Doucet (2008) summarizes, literature on parent involvement indicates that teachers may make (racist and elitist) assumptions about why some parents, such as parents of color or working-class parents, are seemingly "uninvolved" in their children's schooling. Assumptions can then extend to the notion that some parents and families simply do not care about their children. However, in reality, many teacher-child conferences may be scheduled at a time when parents who are working multiple jobs and have inflexible hours cannot attend. Further, some parents and families may not feel welcome for a variety of reasons—maybe no one speaks their mother tongue at school, or maybe they sense a lack of warmth or, worse, racism or discrimination.

The onus is on the educational facilities and teachers to invite families to be involved and accommodate their schedules as much as possible. There may be a cultural and representational mismatch between families and schools, contributing to a sense of alienation. Teachers may lack understanding when child-rearing practices or cultural traditions are different from their own (Doucet, 2008). Preservice teachers must become aware of and interrogate these deficit and at-risk discourses if they are to serve all children and families.

In culturally relevant teaching models, early childhood educators can be encouraged to ask what they can learn from parents, rather than what parents can learn from teachers. Teachers must recognize and validate families' engagement with their children's schooling (Doucet, 2008). To achieve this, teacher education programs may rely on case studies, exemplars, guest speakers, and autobiographical self-reflections to analyze how adults in current or future teachers' lives were involved, and whether this was congruent with traditional models of parental involvement.

In a qualitative study of culturally relevant practices in a preschool classroom, Durden et al. (2015) discovered two common characteristics of teachers who used these practices more often—intentional/consistent connection with families, and previous interactions/exposure to diverse populations. Their study highlights the importance of critical reflection as teachers develop and implement culturally relevant teaching practices. The authors observed a "transformative process" as teachers considered their own cultural identity and their role in including children's cultural experiences into models of best practice.

Early childhood teacher preparation programs can encourage such self-reflection even before educators enter the classroom. Allen and colleagues (2017) published a framework for mapping culturally relevant pedagogy into teacher education programs. While again focusing on elementary and secondary education, the framework applies here in light of the fact that early childhood education is not immune to such issues as institutional racism, inequitable access, and teacher-child cultural mismatch. The authors call out programs that "rely on one-stop-shop diversity classes, glossed-over multicultural training, and ineffective field experiences" (p. 2) as perpetuating implicit biases in future educators. They offer instead a model of critical reflection, social justice action, and critical questions—in other words, teacher education programs that are integrated with culturally relevant pedagogy and (1) pose questions for continual learning of oneself and others, (2) act on social injustices within the education system, and (3) critically reflect on course offerings and instructional practices (p. 14).

Djonko-Moore and Traum (2015) examined the connection between coursework and culturally responsive teaching practices of early childhood teachers and found that neither the number of diversity courses nor teachers' perceptions of their training significantly predicted culturally responsive teaching. Their discussion suggests that the content of diversity coursework be considered in terms of effective impacts on pedagogy. Fortunately, there is an excellent guide for early childhood teacher education programs recently published by Gloria Boutte (2018). After first acknowledging the need for integrative diversity coursework and avoidance of additive approaches, the remainder of the work is dedicated to outlining content and suggestions for developing a foundational course on culturally relevant teaching in early childhood education programs.

Section Summary

Upper-level coursework and field experiences in early childhood teacher preparation programs should provide preservice teachers ample opportunities to apply their knowledge and understanding of children's developing racial awareness and identity. Many paradigms and approaches are available to serve as guides during this process; anti-bias work, critical literacy, and culturally responsive teaching have been included here per their particular relevance to early childhood education.

Suggestion for practice: Provide practicum and field experiences in early childhood teacher preparation programs that garner the necessary skills and opportunities for applying multicultural pedagogies such as antibias, critical literacy, and/or culturally responsive teaching in early childhood classroom settings.

ANALYZING AND EVALUATING BEST PRACTICES

Levels of learning that follow application in Bloom's Taxonomy are *analysis*, *synthesis*, and *evaluation*. Analysis of information includes examining and breaking down content into parts through identification of motives or causes (Anderson & Krathwohl, 2001; Bloom, 1956). Synthesis then involves putting ideas together in a holistic fashion. Lastly, evaluation often requires judgment and critique of information presented. To support these levels of learning in early childhood teacher education programs, let us consider what Beneke and colleagues (2019) describe as an ongoing process of observation, critical reflection, and action.

Beneke, Park, and Taitingfong (2019) developed a framework for teaching and learning about race centered on anti-bias principles and inclusivity. The authors suggest analysis and synthesis of racial knowledge in early childhood classrooms based on identifying entry points (e.g., a comment from a child or a conversation with a family member), wrestling with difficult emotions (anger, hurt, denial, shame), collecting information from multiple perspectives (focused observations, conversations with colleagues), short- and long-term responses, and finally, sharing the process and the product. Through these steps, early childhood teachers can engage in ongoing learning in order to achieve upper levels of Bloom's Taxonomy. Focused observation, critical reflection, and action will enable teachers to continue to evolve as they partner with families to meet the needs of children in their classrooms.

CREATING CHANGE IN POLICY AND PRACTICE

Moving beyond evaluation—the highest level of Bloom's Taxonomy—the revised taxonomy calls for learners to *create*. Equipped with cultural knowledge, empathetic understanding, and tools for ongoing analysis and evaluation of their practices, early childhood educators will be primed for creating change at higher levels. As stated throughout this chapter, *seeing color* in children involves more than awareness—it requires activism rooted in sociopolitical and sociocultural awareness. This is especially pertinent given recent governmental policies and ideologies placing American civil rights at risk.

Furthermore, studies have shown that issues of inequity do not evade early childhood education (e.g., Gilliam et al., 2016). The following NAEYC

(2019, p. 1) position statement calls for professionals to engage in advancing equity in early childhood education:

> All children have the right to equitable learning opportunities that help them achieve their full potential as engaged learners and valued members of society. As a result, all early childhood educators have a professional obligation to advance equity. They can do this best when they, the early learning settings in which they work, and their wider communities embrace diversity and inclusivity as strengths, uphold fundamental principles of fairness and justice, and work to eliminate structural inequities that limit equitable learning opportunities.

Despite professional organizations in early childhood promoting the need for diversity-focused curricula and professional development, most Quality Rating and Improvement Systems (QRIS) developed at the state level have not adequately incorporated elements of cultural competency into their measures. Yet scholars have argued that culturally relevant practices are integral to high-quality early childhood environments (e.g., MacNevin & Berman, 2017).

Early childhood educators graduating from programs that encapsulate the importance of racial awareness, counteracting bias and stereotypes, and continuous reflection of culturally relevant practices will be better prepared to create high-quality environments and interactions that promote optimal development for children from all backgrounds. Going further, early childhood educators and professionals with the requisite training and experience will be positioned to advocate change at regional, state, and national levels that positively impact children and families for generations to come.

REFERENCES

Aikens, N., Klein, A. K., Knas, E., Hartog, J., Manley, M., Malone, L., . . . & Lukashanets, S. (2017). *Child and family outcomes during the Head Start year: FACES 2014–2015 data tables and study design.* OPRE Report 2017–100. Washington, DC: Office of Planning, Research, and Evaluation, Administration for Children and Families, U.S. Department of Health and Human Services.

Aldana, A., & Byrd, C. M. (2015). School ethnic-racial socialization: Learning about race and ethnicity among African American students. *Urban Review, 47*(3), 563–576. doi:10.1007/s11256-014-0319-0

Allen, A., Hancock, S. D., Starker-Glass, T., & Lewis, C. W. (2017). Mapping culturally relevant pedagogy into teacher education programs: A critical framework. *Teachers College Record, 119*(1), 1–16.

Anderson, L. W., & Krathwohl, D. R. (Eds.). (2001). *A taxonomy for learning, teaching, and assessing: A revision of Bloom's Taxonomy of educational objectives.* New York: Longman.

Annis, R. C., & Corenblum, B. (1986). Effect of test language and experimenter race on Canadian Indian children's racial and self-identity. *Journal of Social Psychology, 126,* 761–773.

Apfelbaum, E. P., Pauker, K., Sommers, S. R., & Ambady, N. (2010). In blind pursuit of racial equality? *Psychological Science, 21*(11), 1587–1592. doi:10.1177/0956797610384741

Aronson, K. M., Callahan, B. D., & O'Brien, A. S. (2018). Messages matter: Investigating the thematic content of picture books portraying underrepresented racial and cultural groups. *Sociological Forum, 33*(1), 165–185. doi:10.1111/socf.12404

Aukrust, V. G., & Rydland, V. (2009). "Does it matter?" Talking about ethnic diversity in preschool and first grade classrooms. *Journal of Pragmatics, 41*(8), 1538–1556. https://doi.org/10.1016/j.pragma.2007.03.009

Barbarin, O., & Jean-Baptiste, E. (2013). The relation of dialogic, control, and racial socialization practices to early academic and social competence: Effects of gender, ethnicity, and family socioeconomic status. *American Journal of Orthopsychiatry, 83*, 207–217. doi:10.1111/ajop.12025

Beneke, M. R., & Cheatham, G. A. (2019). Race talk in preschool classrooms: Academic readiness and participation during shared-book reading. *Journal of Early Childhood Literacy, 19*(1), 107–133. doi:10.1177/1468798417712339

Beneke, M. R., Park, C. C., & Taitingfong, J. (2019). An inclusive, anti-bias framework for teaching and learning about race with young children. *Young Exceptional Children, 22*(2), 74–86. doi:10.1177/1096250618811842

Bigler, R. S. (1999). The use of multicultural curricula and materials to counter racism in children. *Journal of Social Issues, 55*(4), 687–705.

Blaisdell, B. (2005). Seeing every student as a 10: Using Critical Race Theory to engage white teachers' colorblindness. *International Journal of Educational Policy, Research, and Practice: Reconceptualizing Childhood Studies, 6*(1), 31–50.

Blanchard, S. B., Coard, S. I., Hardin, B. J., & Mereoiu, M. (2019). Use of parental racial socialization with African American toddler boys. *Journal of Child and Family Studies, 28*(2), 387–400.

Bloom, B. (1956). *Taxonomy of educational objectives; The classification of educational goals, by a committee of college and university examiners.* New York: Longmans, Green.

Boutte, G. S. (2018). Taking culturally relevant teaching to the big house: Implications for early childhood teacher educators. *New Educator, 14*(2), 171–184. doi:10.1080/1547688X.2018.1426327

Boutte, G. S., Lopez-Robertson, J., & Powers-Costello, E. (2011). Moving beyond colorblindness in early childhood classrooms. *Early Childhood Education Journal, 39*(5), 335–342. doi:10.1007/s10643-011-0457-x

Brown, S., Souto-Manning, M., & Tropp Laman, T. (2010). Seeing the strange in the familiar: Unpacking racialized practices in early childhood settings. *Race Ethnicity and Education, 13*(4), 513–532.

Bullock, J. R. (1996). Early childhood educators' beliefs and practices of anti-bias curriculum in rural areas. *Early Child Development and Care, 126*(1), 1–13.

Byrd, C. M. (2012). The measurement of racial/ethnic identity in children. *Journal of Black Psychology, 38*, 3–31.

Caughy, M. O., Nettles, S. M., & Lima, J. (2011). Profiles of racial socialization among African American parents: Correlates, context, and outcome. *Journal of Child and Family Studies, 20*(4), 491–502.

Clark, K. B., & Clark, M. K. (1939). The development of consciousness of self and the emergence of racial identification in Negro preschool children. *Journal of Social Psychology, 10*(4), 591–599. doi:10.1080/00224545.1939.9713394

Curenton, S. M., Crowley, J. E., & Mouzon, D. M. (2018). Qualitative descriptions of middle-class, African American mothers' child-rearing practices and values. *Journal of Family Issues, 39*(4), 868–895.

Derman-Sparks, L., & Edwards, J. O. (2010). *Anti-bias education for young children and ourselves.* Washington, DC: National Association for the Education of Young Children.

Derman-Sparks, L., Ramsey, P. G., & Edwards, J. O. (2011). *What if all the kids are white? Anti-bias multicultural education with young children and families.* New York: Teachers College Press.

Djonko-Moore, C. M., & Traum, L. C. (2015). The influence of early childhood educators' teacher preparation and efficacy on culturally responsive teaching practices. *Teacher Education and Practice, 28*(1), 156–176.

Doucet, F. (2008). How African American parents understand their and teachers' roles in children's schooling and what this means for preparing preservice teachers. *Journal of Early Childhood Teacher Education, 29*(2), 108–139. doi:10.1080/10901020802059441

Doucet, F., Banerjee, M., & Parade, S. (2018). What should young Black children know about race? Parents of preschoolers, preparation for bias and promoting egalitarianism. *Journal of Early Childhood Research, 16*(1), 65–79. doi:10.1177/1476718X16630763

Downer, J. T., Goble, P., Myers, S. S., & Pianta, R. C. (2016). Teacher-child racial/ethnic match within pre-kindergarten classrooms and children's early school adjustment. *Early Childhood Research Quarterly, 37*, 26–38.

Dunham, Y., Chen, E. E., & Banaji, M. R. (2013). Two signatures of implicit intergroup attitudes: Developmental invariance and early enculturation. *Psychological Science, 24*(6), 860–868.

Durden, T. R., Escalante, E., & Blitch, K. (2015). Start with us! Culturally relevant pedagogy in the preschool classroom. *Early Childhood Education Journal, 43*, 223–232. doi:10.1007/s10643-014-0651-8

Farago, F. (2017). Anti-bias classrooms: A case study of two teachers. *International Critical Childhood Policy Studies Journal, 6*(1), 7–21.

Farago, F., Davidson, K. L., & Byrd, C. (2019). Ethnic-racial socialization in early childhood: The implications of color-consciousness and colorblindness for prejudice development. In H. E. Fitzgerald, D. Johnson, D. Qin, F. Villarruel, & J. Norder (Eds.), *Handbook of children and prejudice: Integrating research, practice, and policy* (pp. 131–145). New York: Springer. https://doi.org/10.1007/978-3-030-12228-7_7

Farago, F., Sanders, K., & Gaias, L. (2015). Addressing race and racism in early childhood: Challenges and opportunities. *Discussions on Sensitive Issues: Advances in Early Education and Day Care, 19,* 29–66. doi:10.1108/S0270-40212015000001900429

Gilliam, W. S., Maupin, A. N., Reyes, C. R., Accavitti, M., & Shic, F. (2016). *Do early educators' implicit biases regarding sex and race relate to behavior expectations and recommendations of preschool expulsions and suspensions?* Research study brief, Yale University, Yale Child Study Center. https://medicine.yale.edu/childstudy/zigler/publications/Preschool%20Implicit%20Bias%20Policy%20Brief_final_9_26_276766_5379_v1.pdf

Hirschfeld, L. A. (2008). Children's developing conceptions of race. In S. M. Quintana & C. McKown (Eds.), *Handbook of Race, Racism, and the Developing Child* (pp. 37–54). Hoboken, NJ: Wiley & Sons.

Howard, T. C. (2018). Capitalizing on culture: Engaging young learners in diverse classrooms. *Young Children, 73*(2), 24–33.

Hughes, D., Rodriguez, J., Smith, E. P., Johnson, D. J., Stevenson, H. C., & Spicer, P. (2006). Parents' ethnic-racial socialization practices: A review of research and directions for future study. *Developmental Psychology, 42*(5), 747–770. doi:10.1037/0012-1649.42.5.747

Huguley, J. P., Wang, M.-T., Vasquez, A. C., & Guo, J. (2019). Parental ethnic-racial socialization practices and the construction of children of color's ethnic-racial identity: A research synthesis and meta-analysis. *Psychological Bulletin, 145*(5), 437–458. doi:10.1037/bul0000187

Husband, T. (2012). "I don't see color": Challenging assumptions about discussing race with young children. *Early Childhood Education Journal, 39*(6), 365–371.

Kemple, K. M., Lee, I. R., & Harris, M. (2016). Young children's curiosity about physical differences associated with race: Shared reading to encourage conversation. *Early Childhood Education Journal, 44*(2), 97. doi:10.1007/s10643-014-0683-0

Ladson-Billings, G. (1998). Just what is Critical Race Theory and what's it doing in a nice field like education? *International Journal of Qualitative Studies in Education, 11*(1), 7–24.

Ladson-Billings, G. (2019, August 9). Interview by Laura Fay [online]. 74 Interview: Researcher Gloria Ladson-Billings on culturally relevant teaching, the role of teachers in Trump's America and lessons from her two decades in education research. The 74. https://www.the74million.org/article/74-interview-researcher-gloria-ladson-billings-on-culturally-relevant-teaching-the-role-of-teachers-in-trumps-america-lessons-from-her-two-decades-in-education-research/

Lesane-Brown, C. L., Brown, T. N., Tanner-Smith, E. E., & Bruce, M. A. (2010). Negotiating boundaries and bonds: Frequency of young children's socialization to their ethnic/racial heritage. *Journal of Cross-Cultural Psychology, 41*(3), 457–464. doi:10.1177/0022022109359688

Lewison, M., Flint, A. S., & Van Sluys, K. (2002). Taking on critical literacy: The journey of newcomers and novices. *Language Arts, 79*(5), 382–392.

Loyd, A. B., & Gaither, S. E. (2018). Racial/ethnic socialization for white youth: What we know and future directions. *Journal of Applied Developmental Psychology, 59*, 54–64.

MacNevin, M., & Berman, R. (2017). The Black baby doll doesn't fit the disconnect between early childhood diversity policy, early childhood educator practice, and children's play. *Early Childhood Development and Care, 187*(5–6), 827–839. http://dx.doi.org/10.1080/03004430.2016.1223065

Marcelo, A. K., & Yates, T. M. (2019). Young children's ethnic-racial identity moderates the impact of early discrimination experiences on child behavior problems. *Cultural Diversity & Ethnic Minority Psychology, 25*(2), 253–265.

McIntosh, P. (1989, July/August). White privilege: Unpacking the invisible knapsack. *Peace and Freedom*, 10–12.

McIntosh, P. (2012). Reflections and future directions for privilege studies. *Journal of Social Issues, 68*(1), 194–206.

Miller-Cotto, D., & Byrnes, J. P. (2016). Ethnic/racial identity and academic achievement: A meta-analytic review. *Developmental Review, 41*, 51–70.

Milner, H. R. (2012). Losing the color-blind mind in the urban classroom. *Urban Education, 47*(5), 868–875. doi:10.1177/0042085912458709

National Association for the Education of Young Children (NAEYC). (2019). *Advancing Equity in Early Childhood Education: Position Statement*. https://www.naeyc.org/sites/default/files/globally-shared/downloads/PDFs/resources/position-statements/naeycadvancingequitypositionstatement.pdf

Pahlke, E., Bigler, R. S., & Suizzo, M. A. (2012). Relations between colorblind socialization and children's racial bias: Evidence from European American mothers and their preschool children. *Child Development, 83*(4), 1164–1179. doi:10.1111/j.1467-8624.2012.01770.x

Park, C. C. (2011). Young children making sense of racial and ethnic differences: A sociocultural approach. *American Educational Research Journal, 48*(2), 387–420. doi:10.3102/0002831210382889

Patterson, M. M., & Bigler, R. S. (2006). Preschool children's attention to environmental messages about groups: Social categorization and the origins of intergroup bias. *Child Development, 77*(4), 847–860.

Ramsey, P. G. (2004). *Teaching and learning in a diverse world* (3rd ed.). New York: Teachers College Press.

Rivas-Drake, D., Syed, M., Umaña-Taylor, A., Markstrom, C., French, S., Schwartz, S. J., & Lee, R. (2014). Feeling good, happy, and proud: A meta-analysis of positive ethnic-racial affect and adjustment. *Child Development, 85*(1), 77–102.

Souto-Manning, M., & Cheruvu, R. (2016). Challenging and appropriating discourses of power: Listening to and learning from early career early childhood teachers of color. *Equity & Excellence in Education, 49*(1), 9–26.

Summer, M. (2014). "You are a racist": An early childhood educator's racialized awakening. *The Social Studies, 105*(4), 193–200. doi:10.1080/00377996.2014.894903

Trawick-Smith, J. (2018). *Early childhood development: A multicultural perspective* (7th ed.). New York: Pearson.

U.S. Department of Health and Human Services. Administration for Children and Families, Office of Head Start. (2018). *Revisiting and updating the multicultural principles for Head Start programs serving children ages birth to five*. https://eclkc.ohs.acf.hhs.gov/sites/default/files/pdf/principles-01-10-revisiting-multicultural-principles-hs-english_0.pdf

University of Pittsburgh School of Education, Race and Early Childhood Collaborative. (2016). *Positive racial identity development in early education: Understanding PRIDE in Pittsburgh*. Pittsburgh, PA: University of Pittsburgh.

Van Ausdale, D., & Feagin, J. (2001). *The first r: How children learn race and racism.* Lanham, MD: Rowman & Littlefield.

Vittrup, B. (2016). Early childhood teachers' approaches to multicultural education and perceived barriers to disseminating anti-bias messages. *Multicultural Education, 23,* 37–41.

Vittrup, B. (2018). Color blind or color-conscious? White American mothers' approaches to racial socialization. *Journal of Family Issues, 39*(3), 668–692. doi:10.1177/0192513X16676858

Wang, M. T., Henry, D. A., Smith, L. V., Huguley, J. P., & Guo, J. (2020). Parental ethnic-racial socialization practices and children of color's psychosocial and behavioral adjustment: A systematic review and meta-analysis. *American Psychologist, 75*(1), 1–22. doi:10.1037/amp0000464

Wang, M. T., Smith, L. V., Miller-Cotto, D., Huguley, J. P. (2020). Parental ethnic-racial socialization and children of color's academic success: A meta-analytic review. *Child Development, 91*(3), e528–e544. doi:10.1111/cdev.13254

Whitebook, M., McLean, C., Austin, L. J. E., & Edwards, B. (2018). Early Childhood Workforce Index—2018. Berkeley, CA: Center for the Study of Child Care Employment, University of California, Berkeley. http://cscce.berkeley.edu/topic/early-childhood-work-force-index/2018/

Williams, A., & Steele, J. R. (2019). Examining children's implicit racial attitudes using exemplar and category-based measures. *Child Development, 90*(3), e322–e338.

Williams, J. E., & Roberson, J. K. (1967). A method for assessing racial attitudes in preschool children. *Educational and Psychological Measurement, 27*(3), 671–689.

Zucker, J. K., & Patterson, M. M. (2018). Racial socialization practices among white American parents: Relations to racial attitudes, racial identity, and school diversity. *Journal of Family Issues, 39*(16), 3903–3930.

Chapter Two

Addressing lgbtq+ Issues With Preservice Teachers in Conservative Spaces

Kenya E. Wolff and Janice Kroeger

Ethan got into our small SUV and said hi with lack of enthusiasm that's pretty typical of a middle schooler at the end of a long day. Since starting at his new school, I'd watched my son go from a sweet, enthusiastic, talkative, and generally happy child to a more sullen one. We had moved from a large city to a smaller rural town. Fitting in was proving harder for Ethan than I'd hoped. Earlier in the year, Ethan told me his classmates had told him that he was going to hell because he'd opted out of going to the Fellowship of Christian Athletes meeting at his public school that took place weekly during his homeroom time. Even his teacher had approached him and made Ethan feel guilty for not going.

At the beginning of the year, Ethan had made the mistake of wearing skinny jeans. Boys taunted him, calling him gay . . . which he'd simply shrugged off, saying, "So what? . . . There's nothing wrong with being gay, my sister is gay." Things went from bad to worse after that. He was constantly approached by classmates with comments ranging from "my parents would never let me hang out with you" to "your sister is going to hell and you are too if you don't say being gay is a sin." At one point, a kid sitting next to him in class asked, "What would you do if you saw two boys kissing?" He replied, "The same thing I'd say if I saw a boy and a girl kissing . . . get a room, PDA is gross." That answer didn't satisfy his classmate, who teased him for the remainder of the year.

It had been a rough year, but it was almost over. In fact, it was the next-to-last day of school. That should be reason enough for some excitement, but Ethan was far from happy. Something was off. That's when I saw it . . . it was crème-colored with bold blue lettering. It was torn and tattered but recognizable. On the spine, I made out the words, *Holy Bible*. It took some time before Ethan was ready to share with me why he was carrying it. When the story spilled out of him later that night, it was almost too ironic for me to believe. These same boys who were so worried about his soul had taken that hardbound Bible and used it as a weapon and no, not as a metaphorical type weapon. They wanted to make sure he understood that kids who believe that being gay is okay go to hell. They believed they were doing God's work.

This example shows a mother contemplating the bullying her son had endured at the hands of his classmates. Kenya Wolff knew that this was minor compared to what many students and families who identify as lesbian, gay, bisexual, and/or transgender (lgbt) face daily. As a professor, Wolff is responsible for preparing preservice teachers and she felt like she needed to talk more about issues of gender and sexuality with her students. She also knew the majority of her students identified as conservative and Christian, and that they held traditional values toward gender and sexual orientation. In fact, a student had already told her that she planned to be absent on the day that "Working with LGBT families" was on the syllabus because she was completely "against the topic."

In another class, Wolff had been teaching about positive and harmful stereotyping. She would put several groups like immigrants, single parents, Christians, Muslims, welfare recipients, and LGBT families on the board, and asked students to share common stereotypes about each group. She did this in order to unpack and dispel common misconceptions and discuss just how present these groups are in our society. These are the words preservice teachers used to describe some of the stereotypes surrounding the lgbtq+ community: Diseased, Yucky, Promiscuous, Going to hell, Something to fear, Disappointment, Pedophiles. She was saddened, but not surprised by these words.

Wolff was raised in a home where being anything but heterosexual was considered a perversion. However, through education and exposure to difference, she had learned to challenge her own biases. This proved helpful, because when her daughter "came out," she had learned to challenge her own biases. Thankfully with the help of other educators, friends, and activists who took the time to educate her about this issue, she was able to support her daughter.

Now, as a teacher educator, Wolff was in a position of privilege and wanted to use this to make change, even in the face of the oppressive conditions of the local context. However, she needed to learn more about how to create safe spaces where difficult conversations could exist without turning students off before they were engaged. This was especially important because in the setting in which Wolff worked, the deeply red state of Mississippi, things were becoming heated. The U.S. elections of 2016 had emboldened opponents of the progress made on issues of gender and sexuality. The Nashville Statement, released September 2017, by the Council on Biblical Manhood and Womanhood, states that only heterosexuality is permissible (Damico, 2017). It calls people born with intersex conditions "disordered," derides transgender identities as "transgenderism," and makes clear that anyone who is a lgbtq+ person is immoral. More than 150 influential conservative evangelical leaders, half of whom belong to the Southern Baptist Convention, signed the statement.

Steve Gaines, president of the Southern Baptist Convention, and James Dobson, founder of Focus on the Family and a member of Donald Trump's evangelical advisory board, endorsed the statement. Mississippi passed House Bill 1523, which was designed to protect individuals and businesses who *discriminate* against lgbtq+ individuals and/or their families. This law allows people the right to refuse services to same-sex marriage or transgender people. Wolff was concerned that if the passage and support for this bill was any kind of litmus test for local attitudes, then making the case for inclusion and diversity regarding gender and sexuality in education was essential.

Understanding that this narrow view of gender and sexuality hurts children who are forming their own identities during their early years (Kroeger & Regula, 2017), Wolff wanted to know how to create safe classroom spaces to discuss lgbtq+ issues within her rural, conservative community. She also wanted to be able to acknowledge the religious traditions of her students, while challenging the norms that can lead to hostile school climates.

Wolff had so many questions: How can teacher educators navigate conflicts that may arise due to differing religious beliefs? How can they combat heteronormativity and gender bias in early childhood education and elementary school teacher preparation? How can diverse literature play a role in opening spaces? How can this be done without offending students and having them tune out for the rest of the semester?

Seeking advice from someone who has been working on issues of gender and sexuality in a rural, conservative area regarding reflective practices was important. Together, Kenya Wolff and Janice Kroeger have created this reflective chapter as a guide and starting place for helping other teacher educators address issues of gender, sexuality, and lgbtq+ inclusion in conservative spaces.

Opening the chapter as a parent of a child who is coming out as gay, and having experienced her son's bullying at the hands of students in conservative Christian setting, has emboldened Wolff as a scholar to mindfully support her teacher education students to think in new ways about supporting students and their families. Conversely, but with similar motivations, her coauthor Kroeger identifies as bisexual but is also an ally to lgbtq+ children and families in her scholarship.

Like Wolff, Kroeger's work in teacher education has documented the angst and the emotional and analytical thinking required of teachers while supporting gender diverse families in rural, conservative or even urban, progressive experiences (Kroeger, 2001; Kroeger, 2006). The work required to support individuals who are lgbtq+ is complex and has as much to do with analyzing the local milieu for the likely safety and support for the student or family as it does individual strategies that particular teachers can take to challenge the social setting to respond affirmatively to lgbtq+ identities (Kroeger, 2001; Kroeger & Regula, 2017).

The goal of this chapter is to help teacher educators develop new teachers who understand the importance of allying with their lgbtq+ students and families (National Association of School Psychologists, 2014). First, the authors discuss common discourses around gender and sexual orientation in early childhood education, the importance of utilizing inclusive language and up-to-date terminology, and why it is crucial to teach about lgbtq+ issues while also considering the context in which an educator is teaching. Next, they share some reflective practices for working with preservice teachers to utilize personal experience and examine bias related to gender and sexuality. Finally, the authors share strategies known to increase student's knowledge base around supporting lgbtq+ families and gender diversity in their own classrooms.

COMMON DILEMMAS IN EARLY CHILDHOOD

Most of the mainstream discourse(s) in early childhood are guided by the belief that children are "innocent" and that discussing gender and sexual identities with young children is not developmentally appropriate, or is best left to the privacy of the family (Faulkner, 2011). Payne and Smith (2014), studying teachers, noted how troubling the prospect of working with gender diverse children was to elementary educators, attributing teacher fear and anxiety to issues of invisibility, the prevalence of heteronormativity, and associated discourses of children's innocence and naivety (Faulkner, 2011).

Issues of gender, sex, and sexuality combine to provoke teacher anxiety. The lack of understanding of the complex biology of trans students complicates the matter (Gunn & Surtees, 2011). However, Surtees and Gunn (2010) argue that teachers' rationalization that young children are unaware of gender diversity or too young to understand such topics are likely techniques used to avoid having to acknowledge their own discomfort and lack of technique regarding addressing complex topics.

Malins (2017) argues, "It is not whether gender and sexual identities were discussed with children, but rather, *what* gender and sexual identities?" are addressed, and *how*. Mainstream thinking, highlighted by Nielsen and Davies (2008), suggest that "children develop an emotional commitment to their gender as early as 2 years of age and when they arrive in preschool, with many of them already acting, speaking and behaving according to conventional images of gender—though the contents of these images vary considerably according to culture, historical period, social class, ethnicity, age, and individual circumstances" (p. 159).

These conventional ways of representing gender, along binary (male or female) ways of thinking, hurt children who are still forming their own identities during these years. Furthermore, they create a great deal of tension and discomfort for those whose gender development might be considered nonconforming (Sullivan, 2009).

Heretofore, most mainstream versions of gender and sexuality development taught in teacher education rely upon neo-Piagetian or neo-Freudian interpretations of gender, which emphasize the endpoint gonadal (biological) sex as either male or female and the sexual identity expression of heterosexual as the ideal (Ehrensaft, 2014; Gunn & MacNaughton, 2007; Maccoby, 1988; 1990).

Historically, gender development has been regulated and socially produced along binary lines, focusing on either male or female as the acceptable category (Gunn & MacNaughton, 2007; Maccoby 1988, 1990); moreover, an identity consistent with the sex category assigned at birth has been the desired outcome of healthy development. For children whose gender sensibilities are not cisnormative (or consistent with the sex assigned at birth based on physical appearance), the imposition of gender expectations that do not fit with the child's own sense of who they are, can be harmful and anxiety provoking (Birnkrant & Przeworski, 2017; National Association of School Psychologists, 2014).

Older views of gender development have discounted the ways in which gender permanence is interrupted by our newer understanding of brain development and hormonal influences and the kinds of understandings of gender that social equity movements have allowed (Kroeger & Regula, 2017; Kroeger, Recker, & Gunn, 2019; Sullivan & Urraro, 2019). Newer interpretations of gender in the classroom include expanding options for humans as they develop. Biological options such as puberty blockers or gender reassignment technologies are now available to support gender diversity.

A growing body of social supports for gender diverse students also demand that teachers follow updated approaches in schools, such as adapting to student's preferred gender pronoun rather than gender assigned at birth, or supporting school changes in policies to welcome students more fully (Ehrensaft, 2014; Kroeger & Regula, 2017; Mosso-Taylor, 2016; Nutt, 2015). In addition to a much-needed shift for reinterpreting gender, newer approaches to expanding our version of what encompasses a typical family makeup allow for wider expressions of healthy family types (Golombok 2015; Heilman, 2008).

INCLUSIVE LANGUAGE AND THE COMPLEXITY OF GENDER AND SEXUALITY

Sometimes teachers avoid discussions because they are unfamiliar with the "correct" terms to use and/or afraid of using the wrong or offensive terms. Knowing terminology is one of the first steps that advocacy groups for human rights and teaching tolerance suggest for teachers (Human Rights Campaign, 2017). Definitions for gender and sexuality diversity are readily available, as such terms shift with social change. We begin to include such terms in figure 2.1 and the definitions in table 2.1.

Basic terms in the figure were acquired to support faculty and students as teacher educators. However, there are many public use figures and images that can explain the basic differences between gender (how one's body sex and identification is understood) and how one's sexual expression manifests (the attraction and romantic displays one feels for others). Moving away from the gender binary toward gender exploration allows some children to understand themselves more fully.

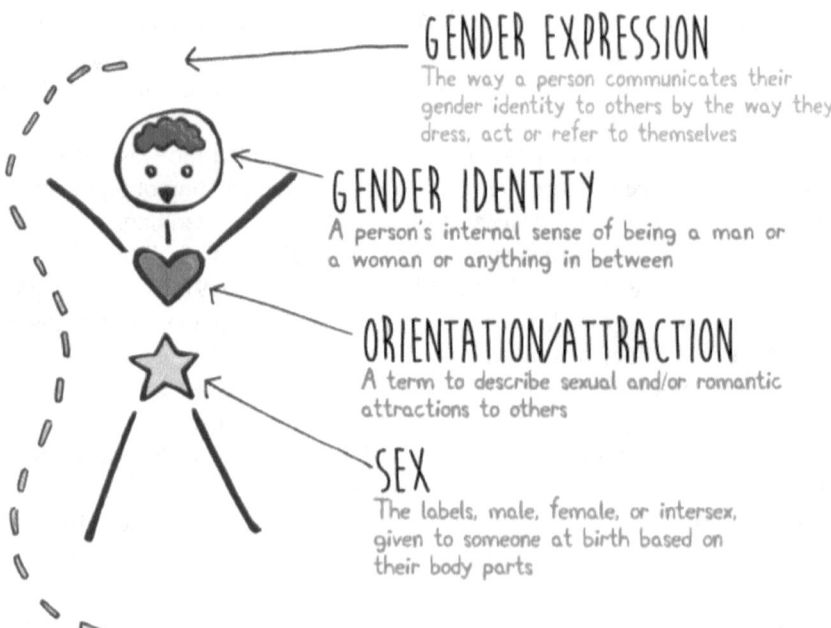

Figure 2.1. Public figure used to explain the differences between gender and sexuality. *Source:* public use.

Why Is This So Important?

Several reforms in traditional teacher preparation programs including early childhood education (ECE) have led to new and increased requirements for pedagogy. Due to these changes there is, in turn, more and more content that needs to be taught in the same (or in many cases, in fewer) credit hours of instruction. How, then, can we expect teacher preparation programs to include and prioritize information about lgbtq+ issues in their curriculum?

It is evident that many teacher preparation programs fail to address lgbtq+ issues (Letts, 2002; Sherwin & Jennings, 2006). This may be done unintentionally because the teacher educators simply aren't conscious of these issues if they do not impact their own identities. Another source of hesitation may be that teacher educators view lgbtq+ issues as difficult or controversial (Gorski, Davis, & Reiter, 2013). Finally, they may refuse to address the issue because of their own anti-gay beliefs (Finnessy, 2007; Sears, 2002).

Regardless of the reason, teacher education programs are perpetuating the status quo and are complicit if they do not address lgbtq+ issues in preservice teacher education programs and do nothing to improve bullying and/or the toxic school environments many lgbtq+ students and families experience (Kosciw et al., 2018).

Table 2.1. Inclusive Terminology

Gender diverse	This term can include individuals who do not neatly fit into the categories of male or female. Gender diversity can include individuals who are transgender, gender fluid, agender, gender nonconforming, or gender expansive.
lgbtq+	This term typically signifies a diverse grouping of individuals representing both gender diversity and sexuality diversity. Commonly an acronym for lesbian, gay, bisexual, transgender, queer/questioning (and other categories such as intersex).
Cisgender	This term signifies a person who identifies with the gender (based on their biological sex) given at birth. This person might be straight, bi, or gay or lesbian.
Transgender	This term signifies a person who does not identify with the gender (based on their biological sex) given at birth. This person might be straight, bi, or gay or lesbian, or polysexual.
Heteronormativity	This term is used to signify the sexual norms of behavior, thought, and social patterns of society, about which lgbtq+ individuals are expected to live, even though their sexual and romantic attractions do not fit a heterosexual life course.

While it can be argued that it is essential for teacher education programs to address lgbtq+ issues, this paper presumes that preservice teacher beliefs and prior experiences regarding these issues are complicated for faculty to navigate and that such issues interact with the course facilitators' own intentions when the curriculum is implemented (Schmidt et al., 2012; Posner, 1992). This is further mired in the faculty's personal and political struggle because students are often encouraged to uncover and express their own biases while challenging oppression and not reinforcing dominant discourses about groups on the margins.

This complicated dance of challenging the status quo while remaining true to the content of disciplinary standards and opening up room for reducing gender bias is a journey that does not guarantee definitive outcomes. Anything can happen in class discussions. Students can mask their own homophobia in subtle but politically correct ways about lgbtq+ individuals, even while at the same time silencing alternative perspectives. Classroom disagreements can stalemate without a faculty member's skill at finding common ground.

LGBTQ+ FAMILIES

The topic of working with lgbtq+ families is challenging to discuss in conservative classrooms. Often programs are quick to discuss "working with diverse families" (including immigrants and families in poverty) but are slow to address support for children in families that identify as lgbtq+. Students with religious views that are opposed to homosexuality can feel threatened when the topic is covered in class, and struggle to negotiate the difference between their own religious convictions and their professional obligation to respect, support, and build relationships with their students' families, which is crucial to academic and social success.

Teacher educators often emphasize the large body of research demonstrating that children do better academically and socially when parents are engaged in their child's school (National Coalition for Parent Involvement in Education, 2006). Furthermore, teachers' affirmation, support, and respect for a child's life experiences, including those having a diverse family structure whether gay, straight, bi, or trans, positively impacts a child's academic outcome and identity formation (Flannery, 2016; Derman-Sparks & Edwards, 2010).

Some opponents of lgbtq+ families might hold the belief that one type of family (the traditional, heterosexual couple with two children) is superior to all others (Heilman, 2008). This belief is harmful, because lgbtq+ families do not fit an ideal heterosexual model, despite their great capacity for raising healthy, happy children (Patterson, 2005). The nuclear American family, referred to as the "traditional family," with heterosexual parents of binary genders (a mother and a father) and children who all live under the same roof has been on the decline for years. Heilman argues that it is the *family ideal* or the family that we "live by" rather than the one that is historically accurate (2008, p. 11).

According to 2010 census data, only 66% of children live in a household with two married parents. This is a decrease from 77% in 1980 (U.S. Census Bureau, 2011). Single parents, blended families, and same-gender parenting in families are on the rise. It is estimated that more than 10 million people have one or more lgbt parents. Many of these children are being raised by a single lgbtq+ parent or by a different-sex couple where one parent is bisexual (Patterson, 2013).

Surprisingly, childrearing among same-sex couples is most common in the South, Midwest and Western regions of the United States, where the highest proportions of same-sex couples raising biological, adopted, or stepchildren include Mississippi (26%), Wyoming (25%), Alaska (23%), Idaho (22%), and Montana (22%). It is noteworthy that Mississippi, Wyoming, Idaho and Montana are considered conservative settings, judging from political voting patterns and by the many rights that lgbtq+ families are denied in adoption, housing, employment, hospital visitation, and other guarantees given to heterosexual individuals in those same states (Gates, 2015).

One of the largest challenges to lgbtq+ inclusivity is that teachers are often uncomfortable with the topic of family diversity, and children and families can feel discomfort advocating for themselves. As teacher educators, we need to provide opportunities for our students to reflect on their own core beliefs about the topic, bring popular myths surrounding lgbtq+ families out into the open, and provide research, anecdotal evidence, and opportunities for reflection.

MYTHS ASSOCIATED WITH LGBTQ+ FAMILIES

There are many myths, misperceptions, and stereotypes about lgbtq+ families. Attitudes and beliefs can be passed on to children and influence how families are treated. Below are some of the most prominent myths associated with lgbtq+ families.

> *Myth:* Children of heterosexual parents are better adjusted than children from lgbtq+ families.
> *Reality:* Research has found that same-sex parents are as effective as opposite-sex parents. In an analysis of 81 studies published between 1992 and 2008, sociologists found *no evidence* supporting the idea that the parenting of opposite-sex parents is any better than same-sex parenting. Additionally, children

of lesbian couples were found to have decreased rates of behavioral challenges and higher rates of self-esteem (Biblarz and Stacey, 2010).

Myth: Teaching about different family types is the same thing as teaching about sexuality.
Reality: Children's interest in family life has to do with who takes care of them, who lives with them, and who they can count on to love them. They notice differences in family makeup and this has nothing to do with the adults' sexual practices. Learning about lgbtq+ families is not much different than learning about heterosexual family structures (blended, step, divorced, etc.). When adults appear uncomfortable or are anything more than "matter of fact" about families and children, students sense it and may feel a sense of shame about their family.

Myth: lgbtq+ people are sexually deviant and will hurt the children in their care.
Reality: The majority of sexual abuse crimes are committed by heterosexual males. There is a large body of research that shows no correlation between child abuse and homosexuality (Herek, 2018). The National Association of Social Workers, the American Academy of Child Psychiatrists, the Child Welfare League of America, and the American Psychological Association all have policies supporting lgbtq+ families and debunking this myth.

Myth: Children raised in lgbtq+ homes will develop inappropriate or confused gender identities and become homosexual.
Reality: Sexual orientation is not passed from parent to child (Farr, 2016; Patterson, 2005). Most lesbian, gay, and bisexual people were raised by straight (heterosexual) parents.

Myth: We don't have any lgbtq+ families in our program/town/school so there's no reason to learn about this issue.
Reality: According to the 2016 Gallup poll, 4.5% of U.S. citizens identify as gay, lesbian, bisexual, or transgender. It is not possible to make assumptions about a person's gender or a family's makeup (even based on appearance or expression) until such a disclosure is given. There is the possibility that a teacher will encounter multiple individuals of lgbtq+ status in either a student's family and/or in the student's identity formation. Teachers have the responsibility to create a respectful, safe, and inclusive environments for all so that families trust us as we work with their students, or determine how and when to "come out" as lgbtq+ (Casper & Schultz, 1999).

Myth: Children raised in lgbtq+ homes are targets for bullying and will be social outcasts.
Reality: There is a long history of discrimination against the lgbtq+ populations and children who are raised by gay, lesbian, bisexual, or transgender parents (Kosciw & Diaz, 2008). However, research suggests that when children perceive their schools and neighborhoods as supportive, they are more likely to thrive (Golombok, 2015; Patterson, 2013; Toomey, McGuire, & Rus-

sell, 2012). As teachers, we can work to make our schools and communities safer and more welcoming for lgbtq+ families.

BULLYING OF CHILDREN WHO IDENTIFY OR ARE PERCEIVED AS LGBTQ+

Multiple researchers have studied the experiences of children and bullying related to gender expression and homophobia. The documentary *Bully* (Hirsch, 2011) is a good resource because it prompts conversation with preservice teachers about the fact that lgbtq+ students report being both verbally and physically harassed at twice the rate of heterosexual students (Human Rights Campaign, 2017). This can further open conversations about the responsibility of teachers to enact anti-bullying policies in their schools and classrooms.

According to the National School Climate Survey (Kosciw et al., 2018), a large number of students who identify as lgbtq+ or who are perceived as lgbtq+ (70.1%) experienced harassment at school based on sexual orientation, and more than half experienced harassment based on gender expression (59.1%) or gender (53.2%). More than a third missed at least one day of school due to feeling unsafe at school, and at least two in five students avoided bathrooms (42.7%) and locker rooms (40.6%). The impact of bullying has been associated with the following negative effects: poor social skills, low self-esteem, physical health problems, higher absenteeism, and social anxiety (Wolke et al., 2013).

Gender nonconforming youth are less likely to finish high school or college, are overrepresented in homeless youth, and more likely to have mental health concerns (Choi et al., 2015). Students who are victimized in schools are more likely to be truant and less likely to pursue higher education. There is also strong evidence that adolescents with sexual minority status (such as transgender, lesbian, gay, or bisexual students) are at a much greater risk for homelessness than their heterosexual peers (Corliss et al., 2011; Ray, 2006).

The good news is that anti-bullying programs and other supports such as counseling, support groups, anti-bullying policies that are inclusive of lgbtq+ students, and Gay-Straight organizations in schools led to less victimization (Hatzenbuehler & Keyes, 2012; Day & Snapp, 2016; Toomey, McGuire & Russell, 2012) and are related to safer schools and better educational outcomes. Yet sadly, lgbtq+ students report that most of these supports are not available to them. That is why teacher educators need to be committed to sharing this information with their preservice teachers.

REFLEXIVE PRACTICES FOR HAVING DIFFICULT CONVERSATIONS

One of the challenges for teacher educators is that students tend to close up during conversations that may be considered controversial. Teacher educators need to create, from day one, a community and environment that appreciates and practices the art of active, empathetic listening. This means setting the ground rules early. Faculty can ask students to write on Post-it notes their thoughts about what would make this class the best ever, then ask students to think back to the worst class they've ever had and write on a Post-it note what would make this class the worse they've ever taken.

Students often share that the best class is one without a lot of high-pressure tests, busy work, or lectures. Students also tend to ask for more class discussions and more activities. Instructors can promise to be organized, lecture less, give fewer high-stakes tests, and create important activities that will help them learn content. Students should also agree to put in some work in order to make this the best class ever. They can create their own rules for the class. A classmate can go up to the front of the class and write down the student ground rules for making this an awesome class. Inevitably, students agree to "be respectful of the teacher and others."

This is a wonderful opportunity, but it can be lost unless there is a deeper conversation about what it means to be respectful. It is in this discussion that students begin laying the groundwork for more complex discussions. The ground classroom rules need to be posted in the classroom and online. It takes months of upholding the ground rules, set on that first day, to create safe spaces.

Once the rules are set, it is important to make sure to talk about the importance of active listening, which is simply the self in the role of the one who is speaking and trying to understand what is being said and what is left unsaid. Stephen Covey (2004) indicates that too often we listen to respond, rather than to truly understand. It is important to remind students to pay attention to the speaker's emotions, body language, and the contexts surrounding the statements made.

Another important strategy to employ is starting with less intense topics around gender and then working up to larger, more uncomfortable conversations. For example, when talking about gender fluidity in the classroom, begin with a simple discussion about the messages sent to children via toy marketing, which reveal hidden bias. After reviewing several commercials in class, it becomes evident that girls are being sold predominately beauty products and boys are being sold violent toys; this is also supported by decades of research (Levin & Kilbourne, 2009; Browne, 1998; Kolbe & Muehling, 1995; Macklin & Kolbe, 1984; Strom Larson, 2001).

Providing examples of commercial messages highlights the gender stereotypes that exist in our society. For example, costumes and clothing can reinforce gender bias, such as in a Halloween costume called "Naughty Leopard" for young girls or a pair of girl's underwear printed with the words, "So many boys, so little time." Belly shirts made for girls that display such messages as "Allergic to homework," "Too pretty to do math," "I'm too pretty to do homework so my brother has to do it for me" all send problematic messages about gender, particularly for young girls.

Similarly, toy commercials allow students to discuss the societal messages being sent to young children about gender, sexuality, and sexism. This can lead to critical conversations about who these gendered and sexualized messages hurt and who they benefit. And, if the facilitator is skilled, these discussions can open up opportunities for even deeper conversations about gender binaries and the social constraints we put on all children.

Children's literature can also be used to provide spaces for conversations about gender and sexuality. Bringing in books that reinscribe traditional gender roles (figure 2.2) can spark conversation, as does comparing these books to ones that challenge these concepts (figure 2.3).

Enforce Ground Rules

Enforcing the ground rules is the facilitator's responsibility, in order to model vulnerability during conversation. Sharing personal stories about lgbtq+ families and gender diverse children can help open up conversations, such as the example at the beginning of the chapter about a child being bullied because of his sister's sexual identity, or sharing classroom experiences about children who were gender nonconforming and needed support.

Personal stories show vulnerability and can help students and teachers connect with other marginalized members of the class. Quiet students can begin to share experiences about being bullied. Often those conversations show the trauma that these students go through; one of Kenya Wolff's students shared that middle and high school had been "a living hell" for him because he had been the target of bullying for his "sissy in Mississippi" ways. When professors share personal stories, often students feel safe to share their own—perhaps not publicly, but privately where they still feel safe.

Advice From Expert Negotiators

In the field of crisis negotiation, there are some key negotiating tactics that professionals use to address conflict. These have been adapted here to address potential conflict or "difficult topics" in the classroom.

Figure 2.2. Sexism in children's books. *Source: I'm Glad I'm a Boy! I'm Glad I'm a Girl!* by Whitney Darrow, Jr., 1970; *How to Be Gorgeous: Smart Ways to Look and Feel Fabulous* by Fiona Foden, 2012; *How to Be Clever: Smart Ways to Get Smarter* by Helen Greathead, 2012.

1. *Pressure creates resistance*: The first step is always to get on the same side of an issue with the students. This doesn't mean that professors reinforce homophobic and patriarchal ideas. Rather, it means express-

Figure 2.3. Children's books that challenge gender stereotypes.

ing support for the ideas that are shared by the class. For example, most teacher candidates enter the field because they genuinely love children and want the best for students and their families. They can agree that teachers need to build relationships with their students' families and demonstrate respect for their students. In addition to these beliefs, they want to create a safe and loving environment for all of their students. Emphasizing the important role of teachers in creating safe and loving environments can reduce resistance.

2. *Reframe the problem*: Change the problem's definition (children are being bullied and parents are feeling disconnected from their school community) to open up the possibility for finding a middle ground. Preservice teachers no longer feel the need to stand their ground and defend their viewpoint, because the question has been reframed. It's not about whether it is "okay to be gay" but rather that there is a serious bullying issue going on in our schools. Students are in school to learn, and learning is prohibitive when faced with aggression and hostility. Therefore, passing judgement on a child or a child's family negatively impacts that child.
3. *Introduce a new solution:* Once we've reframed the problem and preservice teachers have accepted the reframe, we can suggest solutions. At this point, we can introduce the research that physical and verbal assault in our schools needs to be prevented, and that all families deserve a place in their school community. Respect for people isn't about approval. Rather, respect is about creating a school and classroom climate in which every individual is valued for who they are, and can safely achieve academic success.
4. *Develop strategies for remaining respectful:* Sadly, our culture encourages people to remain silent on topics of politics and religion rather than encouraging us to have respectful, in-depth conversations that promote understanding. It is important to learn how to remain respectful to those with whom we disagree while challenging oppression.

Next, we share best practices for how to create safe spaces for discussing gender and sexuality bias as well as heteronormativity in the early childhood classroom. Modeling for students how to be warm, kind, and open even when challenging oppressive ideas is not an easy skill. It can be challenging as a facilitator because there is a fine line between allowing students to unpack and express their own experiences and upbringing while protecting marginalized students from being further oppressed.

One of the best ways to dispel myths is through critical thinking and reflection. Table 2.2 provides some reflection questions that have been adapted from the Gay, Lesbian and Straight Education Network to help students reflect on and deconstruct some of the issues related to serving lgbtq+ families.

Finally, another way we can make sure to challenge oppression is by embedding anti-bias lessons throughout the curriculum. The next section of this chapter will address the practical ways that teachers can support gender diversity and lgbtq+ families in their school community.

Table 2.2. Reflection Questions

Think back to your childhood. What were some of the first things you ever learned about lgbtq+ individuals (positive, negative, or neutral)? Which of those early ideas do you still believe and/or act on? How might your early beliefs impact both yourself and others?

Think about all the things that a child needs, and then consider the characteristics of a good parent. Is our ability to provide for these needs based in our biological sex, our gender expression, or our sexual orientation?

Why do you think it is important to think about lgbtq+ issues regardless of who appears to be coming to your program?

PRACTICAL WAYS TEACHERS CAN SUPPORT GENDER DIVERSITY IN THE CLASSROOM

Educators who utilize the anti-bias approach espouse that "it is not human differences that undermine children's development but rather unfair, hurtful treatment based on those differences" (Derman-Sparks & the ABC Taskforce, 1989, p. 3). When it comes to gender and play within the classroom, teachers should allow children to decide what kind of toys, play activities, and play scenarios they inherently gravitate toward. Children's sense of self may be upset if they feel judged negatively for making the wrong choices in gender expression (Kroeger, Recker & Gunn, 2019). The following are suggestions for educators in their efforts to create gender-inclusive classrooms:

1. *Practice utilizing inclusive language:* Rather than saying, "good morning, boys and girls," use language that opens up nonbinary spaces and provides a sense of community and equity: "good morning class" or "good morning, everyone."
2. *Don't separate children by gender:* When we separate children by gender, we are again reinforcing a binary system that can be uncomfortable for children who identify as transgender or who are questioning their gender identity. This practice places an emphasis on gender as a fixed category. There are several other ways that children can be divided into groups that do not focus on their biological features. For example, they can be grouped according to their pet types, the month they were born, the color of their shirts, or the type of shoes they are wearing.
3. *Feature diversity in books, posters, and textbooks:* All books, posters, and texts should contain a wide range of diversity, including males and females in traditional and nontraditional roles. There are wonderful books that address difference and inclusion, such as *Ogilvy, It's Okay to Be Different, Madam President, A Fire Engine for Ruthie,*

William's Doll, The Princess Knight, Not All Princess Dress in Pink, Knit Your Bit, Ruby's Wish, Ballerina Nate, and *Jacob's New Dress.*

4. *Educate families:* One of the most common concerns parents bring up is the fear that sexual orientation is connected to the types of play a child engages in. Teachers must understand and help parents to understand that there is no type of play that can lead to homosexuality, just as there is no type of play that can undo homosexuality.
5. *Respect children's descriptions of their own identity:* For example, if a child wants to refer to themselves as a "girl/boy" or a "princessboy," be accepting of these descriptions. These self-descriptions should be respected without judgement or correction. Children who are exploring gender expressions may find unique or uncommon ways to define their actions as they grow. Being a "pretend boy" might be the only way a young child who is born male, but feels like a female inside, is able to express the complex social role required to get along in the world if their family is pressuring them to "act male" when they feel otherwise.
6. *Model acceptance of difference:* This should include any differences related to gender exploration and expression. For example, if a boy chooses to wear a dress in the dramatic play area, a teacher's nonjudgmental comment such as "Jack, it looks like you are dressed for an important occasion," can signal to others that it is okay for boys to play at wearing dresses. Children who are gender fluid may persist in this behavior and teachers can affirm, "children can play as they wish in our classroom, because play and dressing are an important part of expressing who we are."
7. *Look for teachable moments:* When teachers overhear children making gendered statements like "boys don't cook" or "only girls wear makeup," they can challenge these stereotypes in ways that are matter-of-fact but nonjudgmental. This can be as easy as challenging these concepts by stating, "my father is an excellent cook" or "I know of a band that is made up of men who wear makeup."
8. *Support children in lgbtq+ families:* Be as inclusive as possible when writing to families in all communication. Rather than "Dear Mom and Dad," use the term "Dear Families" or "Dear Parents/Guardians." Hang a poster or sign that contains your inclusion policy and/or a rainbow flag with the words "We respect all families." Don't assume that a person is "out" and okay with you sharing their living/family situation with others. Finally, get to know the family and learn about the terminology they use with their own children. Support each family's choice regarding how much information they are willing to share (Gelnaw & Brickley, 2010).

9. *Learn how to appeal to school leaders and other allies:* Creating respectful policies for all in educational settings requires working with others in the school. Inclusion of gender or sexuality promotes a safe learning environment for all students. Stand up for a child or family by utilizing or developing inclusive and anti-bullying policies (Kroeger, 2006) such as when a child chooses a new name fitting of their gender identity (Mosso-Taylor, 2016). Finally, recognize that preventing bullying is only a first step in a much wider process of allowing lgbtq+ students to fully participate in a safe school culture where their academic and social educational rights are upheld (Kroeger, 2019).

SUMMARY

As teacher educators, it is our responsibility to ensure that those who enter the field of education are well prepared to be champions for *all* of the families and students they serve. With rising hate crimes against lgbtq+ populations and increased levels of hate speech in our national discourse, the cost of silence surrounding these issues is too great. Teacher education programs must integrate social justice issues of equity throughout the curriculum.

Suggestions for Practice

Critical reflection is needed to help students unpack, detangle, and reflect on their own personal religious beliefs and how they conflict with and contradict their mission to protect and respect their lgbtq+ students and families. Moving beyond reflection, it is our hope that preservice teachers become passionate advocates for the policies and protections lgbtq+ families and students need and deserve.

REFERENCES

Biblarz, T. J., & Stacey, J. (2010). How does the gender of parents matter? *Journal of Marriage and Family, 72,* 3–22. doi:10.1111/j.1741-3737.2009.00678.x

Birnkrant, J. M., & Przeworski, A. (2017). Communication, advocacy, and acceptance among support-seeking parents of transgender youth. *Journal of Gay & Lesbian Mental Health, 21*(2), 132–153. doi:10.1080/19359705.2016.1277173

Browne, B. A. (1998). Gender stereotypes in advertising on children's television in the 1990s: A cross-national analysis. *Journal of Advertising, 27*(1), 83–96.

Casper, V., & Schultz, S. B. (1999). *Gay parents/straight schools: Building communication and trust.* New York: Teachers College Press.

Choi, S. K., Wilson, B. D. M., Shelton, J., & Gates, G. (2015). *Serving our youth 2015: The needs and experiences of lesbian, gay, bisexual, transgender, and questioning youth experiencing homelessness.* Los Angeles, CA: The Williams Institute with True Colors Fund.

Corliss, H. L., Goodenow, C. S., Nichols, L., & Austin, S. B. (2011). High burden of homelessness among sexual-minority adolescents: Findings from a representative Massachusetts high school sample. *American Journal of Public Health, 101,* 1683–1689.

Covey, S. R. (2004). *The 7 habits of highly effective people: Powerful lessons in personal change*. New York: Free Press.

Damico, M. (2017, August 29). CBMW releases coalition statement on Biblical sexuality. Council on Biblical Manhood and Womanhood. https://cbmw.org/topics/news-and-announcements/cbmw-releases-coalition-statement-on-biblical-sexuality

Day, J. K., Snapp, S. D., & Russell, S. T. (2016). Supportive, not punitive, practices reduce homophobic bullying and improve school connectedness. *Psychology of Sexual Orientation and Gender Diversity, 3*(4), 416–425.

Derman-Sparks, L. & the ABC. Task Force. (1989). *Anti-bias curriculum*. Washington, DC: National Association for the Education of Young Children.

Derman-Sparks, L. & Edwards, C. (2010). *Anti-bias curriculum: Tools empowering young children and teachers*. Washington, DC: National Association for the Education of Young Children.

Ehrensaft, D. (2014). Found in transition: Our littlest transgender people. *Contemporary Psychoanalysis, 50*(4), 571–592. doi:10.1080/00107530.2014.942591

Farr, R. H. (2016). Does parental sexual orientation matter? A longitudinal follow-up of adoptive families with school-age children. *Developmental Psychology, 53*(2), 252–264. doi:10.1037/dev0000228

Faulkner, J. (2011). *The importance of being innocent: Why we worry about children*. Melbourne: Cambridge University Press.

Finnessy, P. (2007, January). Queer aporias: Straight teachers and a sexual minority curriculum. Paper presented at the 4th International Conference on Teacher Education and Social Justice, Chicago.

Flannery, M. E. (2016). The power of one: You might be all that's preventing your gay student from dropping out. *NEA Today Magazine*. http:www.nea.org/home/35947.htm

Gates, G. (2015). Marriage and family: LGBT individuals and same-sex couples. *The Future of Children, 25*(2), 67–87. http://www.jstor.org/stable/43581973

Gay, Lesbian and Straight Education Network. (2016). *The safe space kit: Guide to being an ally to LGBT students*. ISBN 978-1-934092-07-1.

Golombok, S. (2015). *Modern families: Parents and children in new family forms*. Cambridge, UK: Cambridge University Press.

Gorski, P., Davis, S., & Reiter, A. (2013). An examination of the (in)visibility of sexual orientation, heterosexism, homophobia, and other LGBTQ concerns in U.S. multicultural teacher education coursework. *Journal of LGBT Youth, 10*(3), 224–248. https://doi-org.umiss.idm.oclc.org/10.1080/19361653.2013.798986

Gunn, A. C., & MacNaughton, G. (2007). Boys and boyhoods: The problems and possibilities of equity and gender diversity in early childhood settings. In H. Hedges & L. Keesing-Styles (Eds.), *Theorising early childhood practice: Emerging dialogues* (pp. 121–136). Castle Hill, NSW: Pademelon Press.

Gunn, A. C. & Surtees, N. (2011). Matching parents' efforts: How teachers might resist heteronormativity in early education settings. *Early Childhood Folio, 15*(1), 27–31.

Hatzenbuehler, M. L., & Keyes, K. M. (2013). Inclusive anti-bullying policies and reduced risk of suicide attempts in Lesbian and Gay youth. *Journal of Adolescent Health, 53*(1), 521–526.

Heilman, E. (2008). Hegemonies and "transgressions" of family: Tales of pride and prejudice. In T. Turner-Vorbeck & M. Miller Marsh (Eds.), *Other kinds of families: Embracing diversity in schools* (pp. 7–27). New York: Teachers College Press.

Herek, G. (2018). Facts about homosexuality and child molestation. University of California, Davis, Department of Psychology.https://psychology.ucdavis.edu/rainbow/html/facts_molestation.html

Hirsch, L. (2011). *Bully* [documentary film]. The Bully Project and Where We Live Films.

Human Rights Campaign. 2017. Glossary of terms.https://www.hrc.org/resources/glossary-of-terms

Kolbe, R. H., & Macklin, C. M. (1995). Gender roles and children's television advertising. *Journal of Current Issues and Research in Advertising, 17*(1), 49–64.

Kosciw J. G., & Diaz, E. M. (2008). *Involved, invisible, ignored: The experiences of lesbian, gay, bisexual and transgender parents and their children in our nation's K–12 schools*. Gay, Lesbian and Straight Education Network (GLSEN). Chicago: Spencer Foundation.

Kosciw, J. G., Greytak, E. A., Zongrone, A. D., Clark, C. M., & Truong, N. L. (2018). *The 2017 National School Climate Survey: The experiences of lesbian, gay, bisexual, transgender, and queer youth in our nation's schools*. New York: GLSEN.

Kroeger, J. (2001). A reconstructed tale of inclusion for a lesbian family. In S. Greishaber & G. Canella (Eds.), *Embracing identities in early childhood education: Diversity and possibilities* (pp. 773–786). New York: Teachers College Press.

Kroeger, J. (2006). Stretching performances in education: Gay activism and parenting impacts identity and school change. *The Journal of Educational Change, 7*, 319-337.

Kroeger, J. (2019). School community partnerships for full inclusion(s) of LGBTQI youth and families. In S. B. Sheldon & T. Taylor-Vorbeck (Eds.), *The Handbook of School-Family-Community Partnerships* (pp. 117–138). New York: Wiley Blackwell.

Kroeger, J., & Recker, A. E., & Gunn, A. (2019). Tate and the pink coat: Exploring gender and enacting anti-bias principles and practices. *Young Children, 74*(1), 83–92.

Kroeger, J., & Regula, L. (2017). Queer decisions in early childhood teacher education: Advocating for gender and sexual minority young children and families. *International Critical Childhood Policy Studies 6*(1), 106-121. http://journals.sfu.ca/iccps/index.php/childhoods/article/view/59

Letts, W. (2002). Revisioning multiculturalism in teacher education: Isn't it queer? In R. M. Kissen (Ed.), *Getting ready for Benjamin: Preparing teachers for sexual diversity in the classroom* (pp. 119–131). Lanham, MD: Rowman & Littlefield.

Levin, D. E., & Kilbourne, J. (2009). *So sexy so soon: The new sexualized childhood and what parents can do to protect their kids*. New York: Ballantine Books.

Maccoby, E. E. (1988). Gender as social category. *Developmental Psychology, 24*(6), 755–765.

Maccoby, E. E. (1990). Gender and relationships: A developmental account. *American Psychologist, 45*(4), 513–520.

Macklin, C. M. & Kolbe, R. H. (1984). Sex-role stereotyping in children's advertising: Current and past trends. *Journal of Advertising, 13*, 34–43.

Malins, P. M. (2017). *Making meaning of gender and sexual identities in early childhood: A critical discourse analysis of Canadian early childhood curricula* [Doctoral dissertation, University of Western Ontario]. Electronic Thesis and Dissertation Repository, Western University.https://ir.lib.uwo.ca/cgi/viewcontent.cgi?article=6368&context=etd

Mosso-Taylor, S. (2016). Humanity, heart, and praxis: Foundations of courageous leadership. In S. Long, M. Souto-Manning, & V. M. Vasquez (Eds.), *Courageous leadership in early childhood education* (pp. 150–162). New York: Teachers College Press.

National Association of School Psychologists (NASP). (2014). *Safe schools for transgender and gender diverse students* [Position statement]. Bethesda, MD: Author.

National Coalition for Parent Involvement in education. (2006). *Research Review and Resources.* www.ncpie.org/WhatsHappening/researchJanuary2006.cfm

Nielsen, H. B., & Davies, B. (2008). Discourse and the construction of gendered identities in education. In N. H. Hornberger (Ed.), *Encyclopedia of language and education* (pp. 910–921). Boston, MA: Springer.

Nutt, A. E. (2015). *Becoming Nicole: The transformation of an American family*. New York: Random House.

Patterson, C. J. (2005). Lesbian and gay parents and their children: Summary of research findings. *In Lesbian and gay parenting: A resource for psychologists* (2nd ed.). Washington, DC: American Psychological Association.

Patterson, C. J. (2013). Family lives of lesbian and gay adults. In G. W. Peterson & K. R Bush (Eds.), *Handbook of marriage and family* (pp. 659–681). New York: Springer.

Payne, E., & Smith, M. (2014). The big freak out: Educator fear in response to the presence of transgender elementary school students. *Journal of Homosexuality, 61*(3), 399–418. doi:10.1080/00918369.2013.842430

Posner, G. (1992). *Analyzing the curriculum*. New York: McGraw-Hill.

Ray, N. (2006). *National coalition for the homeless, lesbian, gay, bisexual, and transgender youth: An epidemic of homelessness.* Washington, DC: National Gay and Lesbian Task Force Policy Institute.

Schmidt, S. J. Chang, S., Carolan-Silva, A., Lockhart, J., & Anagnostopoulos, D. (2012). Recognition, responsibility, and risk: Pre-service teachers' framing and reframing of lesbian, gay, and bisexual social justice issues. *Teaching and Teacher Education, 28*(8), 1175–1184. doi: 10.1016/j.tate.2012.07.002

Sears, J. T. (2002). The institutional climate for lesbian, gay, and bisexual education faculty: What is the pivotal frame of reference? *Journal of Homosexuality, 43,* 11–37.

Sherwin. G., & Jennings, T. (2006) Feared, forgotten, or forbidden: Sexual orientation topics in secondary teacher preparation programs in the USA. *Teaching Education, 17*(3), 207–223. doi: 10.1080/10476210600849664

Storm Larson, M. (2001). Interactions, activities, and gender in children's television commercials: A content analysis. *Journal of Broadcasting & Electronic Media, 45*(1), 41–56

Sullivan, A. L. (2009). Hiding in the open: Navigating education at the gender poles: A study of transgender children in early childhood (Order No. 3361853) [Doctoral dissertation, University of Arizona]. ProQuest Dissertations and Theses A&I. https://search.proquest.com/openview/bd60d8ab992d2c3cb5f454bab16ea26b/1?pq-origsite=gscholar&cbl=18750&diss=y

Sullivan, A. L., & Urraro, L. L. (2019). *Voices of transgender children in early childhood education: Reflections on resistance and resiliency.* Springer.

Surtees, N., & Gunn, A. C. (2010). (Re)marking heteronormativity: Resisting practices in early childhood education contexts. *Australasian Journal of Early Childhood, 35*(1), 42–47.

Toomey, R. B., McGuire, J. K., & Russell, S. T. (2012). Heteronormativity, school climates, and perceived safety for gender nonconforming peers. *Journal of Adolescence, 35*(1), 187–196.

U.S. Census Bureau. (2010). Population Profile of the United States: 2010 (Internet Release). doi: https://www2.census.gov/census_2010/

Wolke, D., Copeland, W., Angold, A., & Costello, E. J. (2013). Impact of bullying in childhood on adult health, wealth, crime and social outcomes, *Psychological Science, 24*(10), 1958–1970. doi: 10.1177/0956797613481608

Chapter Three

Ready for Our Immigrant Children

Preparing Early Childhood Educators to Work With Immigrant Children and Their Families

Wilma Robles-Meléndez

The sun timidly glowed onto the playground of the local school that morning. For the college senior, it was her first day at the school. Her eyes grew big as she entered the classroom for 5-year-olds where she was the assigned student teacher, and met the young children she would help teach. To her surprise, she found a classroom quite different to what she had imagined. She never thought that in this suburban school, she would find such a diverse group of children. Their faces and smiles welcomed her, but she felt intimidated. That was what she later shared in her reflections about her first day.

Most of the 5-year-olds in the class were children of immigrants, including some who had recently arrived and spoke mostly in their home languages. Later sharing her feelings with her college supervisor, she could not help saying, "I want to do my best, but am I ready?"

TEACHING IN A MULTICULTURAL AND DIVERSE SOCIETY

We all want to do our best for the children we teach. Sadly, what the student teacher in this chapter opener experienced is not uncommon. This may be familiar to many who have stepped into a classroom armed with methodologies but not knowing enough about the intricacies of diversity and especially of immigration, with its multiple implications in the lives of children and their families. It is a reality experienced so many times by new teachers, leaving many feeling not competent enough to address the diverse needs of children and families (Tarozzi, 2014).

Some may shrug at what the student teacher experienced and say, "They should know—we already teach them about diversity." The question, however, is what do we teach them about diversity, and how do we prepare them for diversity in their classrooms? Undeniably integral to education, cultures and diversity have become part of the education agenda. The expanding diversity of the student population has been the focus of efforts by multiculturalists who have for years—especially after the civil rights movement—raised awareness about the individual realities and needs of children.

These educators are conscious of the impact of contextual and cultural elements on children's lives and have advocated for culturally responsive teaching practices (Banks, 2015; Ladson-Billings, 2009). Emphasis on multicultural education practices are aimed at creating awareness and building knowledge about the diverse cultures of children and families. In early childhood education, statements about anti-bias and diversity-centered experiences and practices have defined expectations for high-quality, developmentally based practices.

Goals for educational quality and equity remain guiding preparation goals for aspiring teachers and practitioners. Yet, how effectively efforts led to or resulted in knowledge-building experiences about the diverse realities of children and families and on concomitant practices continues to be the focus of discussion by teacher educators, not only in the United States but in the global community as well (Goodwin, 2017; Da Silva Iddings & Reyes, 2017; Tarozzi, 2014; Jennings, 2007).

The Challenge of Diversity

Despite decades of attention to cultural diversity, many teachers continue to express their concerns about feeling "not ready" to face the changing dynamics of diversity encountered in their classrooms (Robles-Meléndez & Driscoll, 2019). Meanwhile, others have decried "their lack of competence to teach in multicultural and diverse classrooms" (Tarozzi, 2014, p. 128). In fact, the challenge posed calls for redefining goals and strengthening learning experiences on the realities of diversity. Current societal trends and the increased presence of learners with varied and diverse realities demand knowledgeable educators capable of responding to the learning and holistic needs of children. This is accentuated when teaching immigrant children, whose experiences may be as diverse as their own cultures are, and who require equitable and responsive attention.

During workshops and sessions, too often we have learned about the frustration of teachers over what was missing from their own teacher training experience. Repeatedly, we have heard early childhood educators point out they realized that learning about the multiple needs of children would be ongoing. They also shared that they never thought they would find themselves facing demands and realities beyond what they learned about diversity.

The fact is that, for most students in teacher education programs, topics related to immigration are not delved into beyond the point of acknowledging multiple ethnic and linguistic groups (Robles-Meléndez & Driscoll, 2019). on more than one occasion, we heard some teachers saying, "this is not what they prepared us to do." Still, despite the challenges, it is important to note how they continue to state, "we care, and want to do our best for children."

Evidently, actions are needed to provide teachers with knowledge pertinent to meeting the needs of a growing diverse population of learners. To make these happen, we determined that changes are critical to prevent the shadow of past misconceptions about people's diversity from continuing to devalue the experiences and needs of children, which could derail the efforts of those who advocate for fair and equitable practices in our classrooms. This is particularly relevant, as others have agreed (Abo-Zena, 2018), given that teachers are usually the first and ongoing point of contact for immigrant children and their families, whose hopes lie in what they experience in the classroom.

The next sections of this chapter further examine facts about immigration as a process and its realities, which support the need for attention to the diverse experiences and requirements of immigrant children in teacher education.

IMMIGRATION—A FACET OF DIVERSITY

With unceasing and increasing immigration, immigrant children are present in almost every community and classroom. Immigration, an elemental characteristic of American society, has been a primary factor contributing to the nation's multicultural and diverse character. Today's classrooms are a complex mosaic of ethnicities, cultures, and experiences, where immigration, among other factors, increases the diversity of the nation's schools. The many languages spoken by immigrant children and the myriad of worldviews evidence their presence in public centers and schools. Given the continual immigration to the United States, the nation's diverse children and their families demand attention in education.

Recently, immigration has also emerged as a topic generating discussions and arguments that distort its value and role in society. The core of these conversations reveal unclear and unfounded notions about what immigration entails for the nation. Many of these views are still influencing practices and attitudes. This fact further supports the need for attention to issues of immigration in teacher preparation and professional development. Counteracting negative and misleading views about immigrants is essential in promoting the value of what people bring to our communities and classrooms.

Immigration Is a Societal Process

Immigration is an integral societal phenomenon and process. The movement of people across international borders has been one of the fundamental actions defining humanity. Many reasons motivate people to migrate, leaving their homelands to seek new places where they can prosper and have a future (Suárez-Orozco & Suárez-Orozco, 2001). As a major change force shaping the societal and historical landscape of countries around the world, immigration remains an active factor in the 21st-century global panorama. News about the arrival of immigrant groups, families, and children have brought the topic to everyone's attention, and many times people take sides without considering the human aspects inherent to immigration decisions. Behind the faces of immigrants are a thousand stories, which hold in common the aspiration for a better life and future.

Difficult and tragic incidents have also shifted conversations toward the realities of immigrant children. In 2017, the United Nations Children's Fund (UNICEF) reported 30 million children worldwide were immigrants "living in other countries different from their place of birth" (United Nations Children's Fund, 2018). With the United States continuing to be a main destination for immigrants, many of these children are in our schools and classrooms, which calls for understanding and a responsive approach.

This Is a Nation of Immigrants

American society and history is a testimonial to the stories and labor of immigrants. Today, its immigrant trajectory continues to be highlighted, as people from practically every culture throughout the world call the United States home (Zong, Batalova, & Burrows, 2019). Many more continue to arrive daily through its borders, both officially and unofficially. Opinions about immigration vary, but despite the tone of arguments in recent years, immigrants are viewed favorably in the United States (Radford, 2019) as they bring their skills and knowledge, contributing to the growth and future of the country.

Annually, it is estimated that nearly a million people officially enter the United States as immigrants (U.S. Bureau of the Census, 2019). The main regions of origin demonstrate the continuing diversity of immigrants living in the United States (figure 3.1). In 2018, 28% of the nation's population were immigrants, a figure projected to increase to 36% by 2065 (Zong, Batalova, & Burrows, 2019). Many are families with children coming in search of their dreams and of a future. According to projections, one in three American citizens will be an immigrant or will be born to immigrant parents (Cohn, 2015). Implications for education are evident, and continue to underline the need for responsive and appropriate teacher preparation (Goodwin, 2017).

In recent years, the strong immigrant heritage of the United States has become more distinctive. Waves of immigration since 1965—the year that the most recent immigration act was passed (Gjelten, 2015)—have transformed the country's demographics. Since then, the presence of immigrants has significantly defined the character of thousands of cities.

IMMIGRANTS IN OUR CLASSROOMS

As the nation's population continues to grow, particularly since 2010, immigration has resurfaced for educators as a reality calling for further attention. The crisis during the summer of 2014, when thousands of unaccompanied children came through the southern borders, led to a resurgence of attention to immigrant children (Rappleye, 2014; Wolgin & Kelley, 2014). Unfortunately, it also brought to light rising anti-immigrant sentiment (Miller, 2019), which has underlined the need for clarity about the factors leading families and children to immigrate.

The focus on children has heightened given the numbers of those arriving in the United States. For educators, responding to the needs of a growing ethnically and culturally diverse student population remains a challenge in need of determined actions. One-quarter of students in American classrooms are children with immigrant roots (Child Trends, 2018), with further growth of the immigrant population indicated in the decades ahead (Radford, 2019; Zong, Batalova, & Burrows, 2019). For example, by 2014, both Hispanic and Asian students had increased their presence in schools throughout the country (National Center for Education Statistics, 2017). Their diverse heritage and cultures are evident in many communities and classrooms. Changing student populations continue to highlight the need for adequate preparation for teachers. The question remains: Are we ready to equitably support and

Figure 3.1. Main regions of origin of immigrants living in the United States, 2017. *Source:* Adapted from Pew Research Center (2020).

respond to the needs of growing numbers of immigrant children and their families?

Fulfilling the Dreams of Immigrant Children

Similar to what the student teacher encountered in the introduction to this chapter, countless educators of young children find themselves wanting to do their best, yet feeling unprepared by not having all the tools for teaching in today's culturally diverse classrooms. Many more will continue to feel the same way as they teach the diverse student populations in schools throughout the nation. The challenge becomes a hurdle when a large majority of children in many classrooms are immigrants. Already, about one-quarter of children under age six in the United States are children of immigrants (Migration Policy Institute, 2019).

Throughout the nation, immigrant families continue to place their hopes in education for a better life for their children. For them, education is the door to reaching opportunities and a hopeful future. In fact, most families would say that one of the main motivations to immigrate was for educational opportunities for their children. Their hopes for a future are centered on what their children will find in our schools and programs. We cannot let down their hopes.

CALLING FOR EQUITY-ORIENTED TEACHER PREPARATION

Central to the successful educational journey of young immigrant children are the educators and the quality of the teaching. Quality teaching entails how responsively teachers provide and attend to education to ensure equitable attention to the needs of the learners, inclusive of their distinct and diverse cultures and experiences (Robles-Meléndez, 2018).

In times where the nature of the classroom is marked by increasing diversity, it is critical to consider if we are preparing teachers to work with a population of children with multiple cultures, languages, and individual experiences.

The call for preparation is aimed at supporting and enhancing teaching quality, teaching that is mindful of the nature and needs of children in our classrooms. As Hollins (2011) pointed out, "Teaching is a complex and multidimensional process that requires deep knowledge and understanding in a wide range of areas and the ability to synthesize, integrate, and apply this knowledge in different situations, under varying conditions, and *with a wide diversity of groups and individuals*" (p. 395; emphasis added).

Echoing Hollins's words, responses to the already diverse reality of classroom enrollment across all levels calls for the integrity of teacher preparation, anchored in knowledge and leading to ways to address the myriad diversity and realities of students. Hollins further cautions that "quality teaching is unequally distributed" (2011, p. 395). Her statement reveals the urgent need for preparation that empowers educators to deliver quality teaching irrespective of the setting. This further underlines issues of equity in teaching experiences and opportunities.

A matter of fairness and social justice, teacher preparation calls for centering expectations on issues that reflect the current realities of the nation's children. A "one size fits all" type of education cannot meet expectations because it denies immigrant children as well as those with other realities of their right to equitable, quality experiences. Instead, an equity-oriented perspective is central to fulfilling our commitment to provide children in our classrooms the best response to their needs and realities.

Today, teacher preparation programs are being called on to more effectively empower teacher candidates and practitioners to address the diverse realities of immigrant children and families. Bollin (2007) pointed out the need for preparation targeted at enabling early childhood educators to effectively work with immigrant students. Similarly, Goodwin's research (2017) outlined the need to prepare educators capable of responding to immigrant students with adequate knowledge and skills. Calls for action are grounded on the fact that many "practitioners do not feel well-prepared to handle effectively diversity issues" (Burns, 2009) since common notions about diversity fail to reflect the existing realities. While teacher preparation programs genuinely consider that diversity is essential to program experiences, outcomes have shown a need for reconceptualizing experiences guided to build the necessary experiences and knowledge that corresponds to the nature of children in culturally diverse communities (Ray, Bowman & Robbins, 2006).

Today's classrooms have become more visibly defined by the multicultural nature of their communities. While there are other factors influencing the ethnic and linguistic characteristics of these communities, immigration has been a pivotal factor in our classrooms.

Some states have seen their population dramatically changed as immigration continues to drive families to places not traditionally known as immigrant destinations (Radford, 2019; Elliott, 2018). Meanwhile, the numbers and magnitude of the immigrant student population continue to demand equitable practices. The resulting demographic impact of immigration on centers and schools accentuates the need for teaching and learning practices anchored in culturally responsive strategies.

Increasing Presence of Immigrant Children in Our Classrooms

A symphony of children's voices, speaking multiple languages and coming from diverse cultures characterize schools and programs throughout the country. These are the children of immigrants, most of whom were born in the United States (Capps et al., 2015). Overall, 23% of students across the nation in 2017 were children of immigrants, reflecting a significant increase from 11% reported in 1990 (Dinan, 2017). Almost 10% of students are speakers of languages other than English (McFarland et al, 2019).

With them, the future of the nation continues to grow and unfold. More than 840,000 immigrant students were attending public schools across the nation in 2014 (U.S. Department of Education, 2014). Meanwhile, enrollment of immigrant children in preschool programs continues to increase. Head Start, a federally funded early childhood program serving almost a million children, reported that in 2018, 37% of the enrollment were Hispanic children (Head Start, 2019). Twenty-seven percent of 3- to 4-year-olds attending Head Start were children with Asian roots in 2014 (Child Trends, 2015), which further highlights the growing ethnic diversity of children and families attending preschool programs.

Beyond the demographics, experiences have made evident the many factors and different challenges facing immigrant children, which place their opportunities for educational and life success at risk. Emphasis on the realities of immigrant children and their families is critical for educators working in immigrant communities, as these contribute to building awareness and understanding about the challenges these families face.

Key to addressing the issues of immigrants is the need for demystifying views and preconceived ideas and perceptions about immigrant children, such as a "deficit-oriented perspective" (Da Silva Iddings & Reyes, 2017, p. 34) about their heritage and culture. Reports continue to show that enrollment of young immigrant children in preschool programs lags, challenging their schooling success (Robles-Meléndez & Beck, 2019; Golden & Fortuny, 2010; Keels & Raver, 2009).

Despite countless success stories about immigrant families, many immigrant children live in poverty and lack essential services. There are many reasons for this. Access and information about existing services and early intervention programs fails to reach all families. Lack of awareness about programs and services coupled with fear due to immigration status deters and prevent countless immigrant parents from participating in what they are entitled to receive. Lingering discrimination and prejudice add to their challenges and risks. The harm these bring remains an obstacle that underlines the need for practices geared at counteracting the damage and ending their impacts on everyone.

Building Teacher Knowledge About Immigration

Immigration is a complex process and experience for children and families. There are always exceptions but, as pointed out earlier, much about immigration is not typically addressed in teacher preparation. This void is evidently left to be filled through one's experiences or what one may learn by working with immigrant children and their families. This is what many teachers continue to do today.

Robles-Meléndez and Driscoll (2019) asked a group of experienced early childhood teachers about their work in mostly ethnically diverse settings. It was evident in their answers that they showed care and attention for the children. However, the teachers' responses demonstrated the lack of knowledge about immigrant children and their families. Some observed that they had some notions but no firm knowledge about immigration or its impact on families. Others had been unaware of the existing rights or educational services for immigrants, most of which they had learned while working with children.

While the teachers' commitment to children was evident based on their efforts and stories of remarkable deeds, the tools provided during their preparation and professional development is a source of concern. It is irrefutable that experiences encountered in the field are a powerful ongoing learning tool for sharpening and refining ideas. However, it is equally undeniable that today there is a need for a strong and balanced knowledge base aimed at preparing educators to respond to a socially diverse student community. We are in a time when awareness of what is socially just calls for actionable steps. The challenge is answering to the needs of young children and their families in equitable and responsive ways. Preparing early childhood educators is undeniably a priority in society.

Arming educators with the tools of knowledge and sensitivity to address the realities of immigrant children and their families is critical. If we are give children equal opportunities, effective and duly responsive experiences are vital. Key to making achieving this is training aspiring early educators and providing professional development of practitioners (Golden & Fortuny, 2010).

FAILING THE DREAM OF EQUALITY

All children deserve and are entitled to education that is equitable, irrespective of their ethnic and cultural characteristics or immigration status. With the foundational and critical role of early childhood education, this is what also guides the work of educators of young children. Central to delivering and fulfilling this mission of an equitable education is the professional preparation of the nation's teaching force. Yet, the question remains if their training adequately responds to the needs of the current student population for whom immigration is one of their many realities (Goodwin, 2017).

We need to close the gaps in teacher preparation, particularly those that challenge the dream of educational equality (Bollin, 2007; Robles-Meléndez & Beck, 2019). Responsively attending to what is fair and equitable for every child is the hallmark of education. It is also at the core of what defines socially responsible and just actions toward children. However, this was not the common denominator for thousands of immigrant children who found themselves in classrooms. Many still fondly remember teachers whose sense of empathy and professionalism moved them to do the impossible despite finding themselves learning along with their students. Yet there were, and are, many others whose experiences continue to hurt (Suárez-Orozco & Suárez-Orozco, 2001). Those are memories that never go away. For example, a director of an early childhood center shared with the author how she still remembers the derogatory labels she was called.

Today we cannot simply rely on the goodwill, best intentions, and dedication of educators, as this would be unfair to them. They continue to act with integrity and sincere commitment to children, but of quality and informed practices cannot happen when appropriate preparation lags behind. This is what Goodwin (2017) denounced when her study revealed that little had changed since 2002 in preparing teachers to address the needs of immigrant children. Her analysis of the literature on teacher preparation showed that, though some efforts have been made, the vacuum in teacher training regarding immigrant children was still evident.

Though recent data shows a slower rate of immigration to the United States (Tavernise, 2019), projections continue to indicate a steady growth of immigrants into the coming decades, particularly in states such as Texas, Florida, and Arizona. Aside from those states that have traditionally served as immigrant destinations, many others like South Carolina, Alabama, Tennessee, and Georgia have become home for thousands of families from other countries (Elliott, 2018; Terrazas, 2011). In many cities across the country, the immigrant population has jumped or changed the demographic nature of schools and communities (table 3.1).

In some school districts, as in the case of Miami-Dade in Florida and Clarks County in Nevada, the immigrant student population has become a majority. As such, the need for teachers' sound knowledge and experience working with culturally and linguistically diverse learners remains a priority.

Perreira and Ornelas (2011) indicate that professionals seeking the physical and psychological well-being of immigrant children "must improve their understanding of the unique experiences of immigrant children" (p. 195). Simply stated, what we know makes a difference in how we respond to the needs of our immigrant children and their families. It is a matter of forming a solid knowledge base to better prepare educators for informed decisions in their classrooms (Robles-Meléndez & Driscoll, 2019). It is also an issue of

Table 3.1. Five U.S. Cities with the Largest Immigrant Populations, 2017

State	City
California	Los Angeles
New York	New York City
Florida	Miami
Illinois	Chicago
Texas	Houston

Source: Adapted from Radford (2019).

equity given the need to ensure equal opportunities and experiences for every child.

IT'S A QUESTION OF PREPARATION FOR DIVERSITY AND EQUITY

Preparation is essential if educators are to successfully address the needs of a growing, culturally diverse student population. The question of preparation becomes even more critical as the profession continues to reaffirm their commitment to children. This becomes particularly clear in the position statement of the National Association for the Education of Young Children (NAEYC, 2019, p. 5).

Equity has long been at stake as an issue of fairness for all children. In a time of increasing diversity, fairness in practices and experiences for children of immigrants remains a challenge (Abo-Zena, 2018). It is also a question, calling us to consider if we are effectively preparing educators of young children to meet and address the multiple realities of immigration. Integral to the issue of responsive practices for immigrant children is the underlying ethical responsibility of doing our best for children.

That commitment also pertains to how we are preparing their teachers to meet the realities of a culturally diverse society. This is what Drake and Flenaugh (2016) emphasized when upholding equity as "the most pressing teacher-preparation issue of our time: preparing educators to teach diverse groups of students." What is more, this is an ongoing challenge for our society. Many educators have already posed the need for appropriate practices to address their students' diversity and particularly to effectively support their educational experiences (Abo-Zena, 2018; Suárez-Orozco, 2017; Goodwin, 2017; Robles-Meléndez, 2018; Gonzalez, Moll, & Amanti, 2005). The issue is one of fairness for both children and their teachers.

However, the nature of the experiences of thousands of young immigrant children in classrooms across the nation remains a challenge to delivering what we know is fair and equitable. Unfair and discriminatory practices, whether intentional or not, have come to the fore and call for concerted action. Responses to the diverse experiences of children and their families have been mixed. While many communities have embraced them, the experience of others has not been as welcoming.

Responding to Contextual Realities

In education, responding to the needs of students has always called for understanding contextual factors and circumstances. Essentially, this means recognizing the needs of the child both individually and societally. Contextual factors are critical to informing pedagogical practices as well as expectations for teacher preparation that will ensure successful educational experiences for all learners so that educational equity and quality are not placed at risk (Hollins, 2011).

Teachers have already expressed concerns about the knowledge tools they bring to the classroom. They have pointed to what we could call "readiness" to respond to the realities of diversity where immigration plays a major role. Knowledge is central to supporting the readiness of the teaching force in addressing the needs of children.

As we prepare teachers to successfully address and respond to an already diverse student population, it is critical to determine how diversity issues are highlighted throughout the candidate's experience. In his study on diversity, Jennings (2007) pointed out the need to understand how diversity issues are presented. He further pointed out how attention on diversity is focused, as it may "obscure other forms of diversity" (p. 1265). With immigration seen as a controversial issue, many times this is a topic avoided or not examined with due rigor.

CONCLUSION

The call for meeting the challenge of teacher preparation that addresses diversity and equity issues of immigrants has been made by many before. Mindful of the challenge, these educators have called for programs to conscientiously answer the need for preparation geared at responding to a diverse population of learners in our classrooms (Abo-Zena, 2018; Suarez-Orozco, 2017; Goodwin, 2017). We simply reiterate their call, in particular, calling for attention to the multiple experiences of young children of immigrants who comprise a large percentage of the nation's students in both public and private schools and centers.

Many may ask: What to do? The answer begins with a position of empowerment to address diversity and equity issues. Robles-Meléndez and Driscoll (2019) pointed to unpacking the factors inherent to diversity and engaging educators to critically reflect on and uncover its implications for young learners and their families. It is through reflection that one transforms what is learned into personal meaning, and sees the dimensionality of diversity factors as they act on individuals.

An examination of the realities of immigration through the perspective of what is equitable in a diverse society is essential for educators to understand their experiences and to more fully build knowledge about immigrant struggles. This is fundamental to addressing prejudice and discrimination. Bringing real-life experience to aspiring teachers and practitioners in order to capture the many eventualities children and families face gives context to what they bring to the classroom. This can also eliminate misleading "deficit" views about their students' cultures and life experiences to equitably address their educational needs and expectations (Goodwin, 2017; Da Silva Iddings & Reyes, 2017; Gonzalez, Moll, & Amanti, 2005). More specifically, from a Freirean position, teacher preparation is aimed at leading educators to become conscientious about the existing inequities (Freire, 1974/2013). In essence, the call is for integrating issues beyond the classroom walls where life's realities give context to the experiences of children.

Over the years, advocates for diversity have provided recommendations to strengthen preparation of education professionals. They have pointed to a variety of instructional strategies that bring the diverse realities of immigrants into the teacher preparation curricular agenda. Most concur with the need for intentionally integrating critical reflection to examine prejudice and issues of inequities and discrimination.

Programs often consider it essential to engage teacher candidates and practitioners in contexts with immigrant children and families. Experiential programs including service learning and intensive internship experiences that lead preservice teachers to mindfully build awareness about the contextual settings of immigrant children and families (Da Silva Iddings & Reyes, 2017; Tilley-Lubbs, 2011). The hope is to create connections with the facts defining the lives of immigrant children in our classrooms.

Suggestions and recommendations to improve the knowledge building of aspiring teachers and practicing educators continue to note the need for broadening views and clarifying misconceptions about immigrants. This is critical to reaching what Takanishi (2004) calls leveling the playing field for immigrant children. While the question of what to do and the call for action remains to be answered, children of immigrants continue to wait for education that duly meets their needs and builds their hopes and dreams.

Action, Please!

Changes are needed if the profession is to close the distance between teacher preparation and the needs of immigrant children. Some changes will take time. While changes to policies and practices are being determined, programs preparing early childhood educators could do several things. The following are some actions that programs can launch to address the immigrant equity challenge.

- Bring the issue to the attention of the faculty. Begin a conversation about what early educators would need to know about immigration and immigrant children. Discuss the challenge from the perspective of equity. The NAEYC position statement on equity (2019) could be a good starting point.
- Engage the faculty in an ongoing conversation and dialogue to identify ways to integrate knowledge and practices throughout program experiences.
- Form an advisory group with practicing teachers, parents, and students with diverse backgrounds and immigrant roots. Learn about their stories and circumstances they face. Invite their comments and suggestions to enhance teacher knowledge.
- Search and learn about what other programs are doing to prepare preservice educators and practitioners about immigrant realities. Contact these programs and begin a dialogue to learn how they responded and more about ongoing responses.
- Lastly, never be discouraged; do not allow obstacles to dissuade your efforts. They will take time, but it will become easier once you get started.

REFERENCES

Abo-Zena, M. (2018). Supporting immigrant-origin children: Grounding teacher education in critical developmental perspectives and practices. *Teacher Educator, 53*(3), 263–276.

Banks, J. (2015). *Cultural diversity and education: Foundations, curriculum, and teaching* (6th ed.). New York: Routledge.

Bollin, G. (2007). Preparing teachers for Hispanic immigrant children: A service learning approach. *Journal of Latinos and Education, 62*(3), 177–189.

Burns, T. (2009, May 29). *Teacher education for diversity* [Paper presentation]. Organisation for Economic Cooperation and Development (OECD), Teacher Education for Diversity experts meeting, Genoa, Italy.

Capps, R. Newland, K., Fratzke, S., Groves, S., Fix, M., McHugh, M., & Auclair, G. (2015, June). *The integration outcomes of U.S. refugees: Successes and challenges*. Migration Policy Institute. https://www.migrationpolicy.org/research/integration-outcomes-us-refugees-successes-and-challenges

Child Trends. (2015). *Head Start*. https://www.childtrends.org/indicators/head-start

Child Trends. (2018). Immigrant children. https://www.childtrends.org/?indicators=immigrant-children

Cohn, D. (2015, October 5). Future immigration will change the face of America by 2065: Fact Tank. Washington, DC: Pew Research Center. https://www.pewresearch.org/fact-tank/2015/10/05/future-immigration-will-change-the-face-of-america-by-2065/

Da Silva Iddings, A., & Reyes, I. (2017). Learning with immigrant children, families and communities: The imperative of early childhood education. *Early Years, 37*(1), 34–46.

Dinan, S. (2017, March 15). Assimilation under threat as children of immigrants flood U.S. public schools. *Washington Times.* https://www.washingtontimes.com/news/2017/mar/15/immigrants-children-numbers-growing-us-public-scho/
Drake, C., & Flenaugh, T. (2016, February 16). Teacher-prep accountability has an equity problem. *Education Week.* https://www.edweek.org/ew/articles/2016/02/17/teacher-prep-accountability-has-an-equity-problem.html?print=1
Elliott, M. (2018, January 31). 10 states where the number of immigrants is growing fastest. Showbiz Cheatsheet. https://www.cheatsheet.com/culture/states-where-the-number-of-immigrants-growing-fastest.html/
Freire, P. (1974/2013). *Education for critical consciousness.* London: Bloomsbury.
Gjelten, T. (2015, October 2). The immigration act that inadvertently changed America. *The Atlantic.* https://www.theatlantic.com/politics/archive/2015/10/immigration-act-1965/408409/
Golden, O. & Fortuny, K. (2010). *Young children of immigrants and the path to educational success: Key themes from an Urban Institute roundtable.* Urban Institute. http://www.urban.org/sites/default/files/publication/27276/412330-Young-Children-of-Immigrants-and-the-Path-to-Educational-Success.PDF
Gonzalez, N., Moll, L., & Amanti, C. (2005). *Funds of knowledge: Theorizing practices in households, communities, and classrooms.* NJ: Lawrence Erlbaum.
Goodwin, L. (2017). Who is in the classroom now? Teacher preparation and the education of immigrant children. *Educational Studies, 53*(5), 433–449.
Head Start. (2019). *Program facts: Fiscal year 2018.* Head Start Early Childhood Learning and Knowledge Center. https://eclkc.ohs.acf.hhs.gov/about-us/article/head-start-program-facts-fiscal-year-2018
Hollins, E. (2011). Teacher preparation for quality teaching. *Journal of Teacher Education, 62*(4), 395–407.
Jennings, T. (2007). Addressing diversity in U.S. teacher preparation programs: A survey of elementary and secondary programs' priorities and challenges across the United States of America. *Teaching and Teacher Education, 23*(8), 1258–1271. doi:10.1016/j.tate.2006.05.004
Keels, M. & Raver, C. (2009). Early learning experiences and outcomes for children of U.S. immigrant families: Introduction to the special issue. *Early Childhood Research Quarterly, 24,* 363–366. doi:10.1016/j.ecresq.2009.09.002
Ladson-Billings, G. (2009). *The dreamkeepers. Successful teachers of African American children.* New York: John Wiley.
McFarland, J., Hussar, B,. Zhang, J., Wang, K., Hein, S., Dilberti, M., Forrest, E., Bullock, F., & Barmer, A. (2019). *The condition of education 2019.* National Center for Education Statistics. https://nces.ed.gov/pubsearch/pubsinfo.asp?pubid=2019144
Migration Policy Institute. (2019). Children in U.S. immigrant families. https://www.migrationpolicy.org/programs/data-hub/charts/children-immigrant-families
Miller, M. (2019, September 23). Immigrant children fill this Minnesota town's schools. Their bus driver is leading the backlash. *Omaha World Herald.* https://www.omaha.com/news/trending/immigrant-children-fill-this-minnesota-town-s-schools-their-bus/article_d22453c3-8f98-5a1d-bc5b-e2bf1e6a16dc.html.
National Association for the Education of Young Children. (2019). *Advancing equity in early childhood education: Position Statement.* https://www.naeyc.org/sites/default/files/globally-shared/downloads/PDFs/resources/position-statements/naeycadvancingequitypositionstatement.pdf
National Center for Education Statistics. (2017). Racial/ethnic enrollment in public schools. In NCES, *The condition of education 2017* (chapter 2). https://nces.ed.gov/programs/coe/pdf/coe_cge.pdf
Perreira, K. & Ornelas, I. (2011). The physical and psychological well-being of immigrant children. *Future of Children, 21*(1), 195–218.
Pew Research Center. (2019). Origin regions. https://www.pewresearch.org/hispanic/2020/08/20/facts-on-u-s-immigrants/#fb-key-charts-origins

Radford, J. (2019, June 17). Key findings about U.S. immigrants: Fact Tank. Pew Research Center. https://www.pewresearch.org/fact-tank/2019/06/17/key-findings-about-u-s-immigrants/

Rappleye, H. (2014, July 9). Undocumented and unaccompanied: Facts, figures on children at the border. *NBC News.* https://www.nbcnews.com/storyline/immigration-border-crisis/undocumented-unaccompanied-facts-figures-children-border-n152221

Ray, A., Bowman, B. & Robbins, J. (2006). *Preparing early childhood teachers to successfully educate* all *children: The contribution of four-year undergraduate teacher preparation programs.* Report to the Foundation for Child Development. Chicago, IL: Erikson Institute.

Robles-Meléndez, W. (2018). *Preparing early childhood educators to meet the needs of our immigrant children* [Group presentation], Table 9: Keeping up with the times summer conference, National Association of Early Childhood Teacher Educators, Austin, Texas.

Robles-Meléndez, W., & Beck, V. (2019). *Teaching young children in multicultural classrooms: Issues, concepts, and perspectives* (5th ed.). Boston, MA: Cengage.

Robles-Meléndez, W., & Driscoll, W. (2019, August 22). *Teacher, I am here! Addressing the well-being of young immigrants through culturally and socially responsive practices* [Paper presentation]. European Early Childhood Research Association, 29th Conference, Thessaloniki, Greece.

Suárez-Orozco, C. (2017). The diverse immigrant student experience: What does it mean for teaching? *Educational Studies, 53*(5), 522–534.

Suárez-Orozco, C., & Suárez-Orozco, M. (2001). *Children of immigration.* Cambridge, MA: Harvard University Press.

Takanishi, R. (2004). Leveling the playing field: Supporting immigrant children from birth to eight. *Future of Children, 14*(2), 61–79.

Tarozzi, M. (2014). Building an "intercultural ethos" in teacher education. *Intercultural Education, 25*(2): 128-142.

Tavernise, S. (2019, September 26). Immigrant population growth in the U.S. slows to a trickle. *New York Times,* https://www.nytimes.com/2019/09/26/us/census-immigration.html#:~:text=The%20U.S.%20population%20gained%20immigrants,seen%20as%20the%20likely%20cause

Terrazas, A. (2011, February 8). Immigrants in new-destination states. Migration Policy Institute. https://www.migrationpolicy.org/article/immigrants-new-destination-states/

Tilley-Lubbs, G. (2011). Preparing teachers for teaching immigrant students through service-learning in immigrant communities. *World Journal of Education, 1*(2), 104–114. doi:10.5430/wje.v1n2p104

United Nations Children's Fund (UNICEF). (2018). *A right to be heard: Listening to children and young people on the move.* https://data.unicef.org/resources/youthpoll/

U.S. Bureau of the Census. (2019). U.S. and world population clock. https://www.census.gov/popclock/

U.S. Department of Education. (2014). *Educational Services for Immigrant Children and Those Recently Arrived to the United States.* https://www2.ed.gov/policy/rights/guid/unaccompanied-children.html

Wolgin, P., & Kelley, A. M. (2014, June 18). 5 things you need to know about unaccompanied children. Center for American Progress. https://www.americanprogress.org/issues/immigration/news/2014/06/18/92056/5-things-you-need-to-know-about-the-unaccompanied-minors-crisis/

Zong, J., Batalova, J., & Burrows, M. (2019). *Frequently requested statistics on immigrants and immigration.* Washington, DC: Migration Policy Institute. https://www.migrationpolicy.org/article/frequently-requested-statistics-immigrants-and-immigration-united-states#Now.

Chapter Four

Religion in Early Childhood

Guidelines for Preservice Teachers

Ruth Vilà-Baños, Montserrat Freixa Niella, Assumpta Aneas Alvarez, and Angelina Sánchez Martí

The Declaration of the Rights of the Child, approved by the United Nations in 1959, includes the right to spiritual development in its second principle. Unfortunately, in subsequent conventions this right received no further mention, as Watson (2009) notes. This omission prompts a series of questions: Why did the right to spiritual development disappear? Has spirituality lost its value for 21st-century society? What role can spirituality and religion play in our lives and, more specifically, in children's lives? Should teachers, including those in secular schools, deal with the subject in the classroom? How?

To answer these questions, we need to bear in mind the prevailing conditions in our globalized world. Education is deeply influenced by economics and politics, especially in OECD (Organisation for Economic Cooperation and Development) countries. The hegemonic system of globalized neoliberalism sees education from a market perspective, in which competition and efficiency are the driving principles. (Casal, Garcia, & Merino, 2007; McInerney, 2004).

This approach can be seen in the gradual change in curriculum design, which has increasingly focused on describing learning outcomes in terms of the knowledge, skills, and attitudes equipping students to acquire the competencies needed for working and living productively in society (Welbourne, 2000). It can also be seen in the stress laid on accountability in assessment systems such as PISA (Program for International Student Assessment), or in assessment processes themselves.

Many would argue that this is the best way to attain high-quality educational outcomes, since a pragmatic, utilitarian approach is what will best equip students for success on the labor market. However, as Souza (2009) and Watson (2009) remark, many educators and teachers are concerned about this bias, in which they see utilitarian goals outweighing other objectives relating to the personal growth and development of children, youth, and the person as a whole.

Generally, research and practice in teacher training focus on technical aspects of the curriculum, teaching practices, and technological support. Only the advent of the inclusive education model has allowed universities and teacher education programs to give attention to educational needs stemming from cultural, socioeconomic, and aptitude differences. Yet inclusiveness has not altered the socio-anthropological vision of humankind prevailing in the academic world, which revolves around biological and psychological attributes of the individual self interacting ecologically and dialogically with the social and natural environment.

Within this socio-anthropological framework and the utilitarian view of education, spirituality is simply ignored. Thus, religious issues only become visible and enter educational praxis through two main postures: secularism and confessionalism. In the first case, all references to religion are avoided so that there is no confusion with religiosity; while the second case adopts a proselytizing model aiming at recruiting converts to the religion in question.

These approaches have not provided valid responses to the existential void felt by postmodern human beings. This is a feeling that can take the shape of a corrosive feeling of powerlessness, accompanied by fear or rage, and has led to the relentless rise of different forms escapism—from addiction, radicalism, and violence to suicide at ever-earlier ages.

In this chapter we set out a series of concepts and precepts as a guide for preservice teachers on how to address religion in early childhood, under the following headings:

- Spirituality and religion: Clarifying the concepts
- Spirituality and religion in the life of the child
- Intercultural and interreligious dialogue in education
- Learning environments for spiritual development
- Teacher education for fostering interreligious dialogue in class
- Promoting interreligious dialogue in early childhood
- Family, community and religion in early childhood

SPIRITUALITY AND RELIGION: CLARIFYING THE CONCEPTS

Spirituality is a vital factor in our lives. Its widely varying definitions show how ambiguous the term can be. Spirituality encompasses various levels of connection with the self and the other (Souza, 2009). The total set of these relationships is what vivifies and shapes every individual's spiritual journey through the course of their life.

When proper spiritual development is addressed, the relationship and balance between self and other play a vital role in the full development of children and youth. Children are particularly vulnerable to the disruptive influence of dysfunctional social and family models. Children need strong family and community roots that will help them with their identity, their sense of being and place, rather than alienation. This is helpful for young people who feel that their lives are worthless or who feel disconnected from their community or society. The experience of alienation that often ensues can cause mental and emotional instability.

In our view, the definition of spirituality offered by the physician and psychotherapist Viktor Frankl helps to clarify these issues. Frankl's long career in clinical practice led him to identify a component of the psyche—always present, sometimes conscious and sometimes not, which was substantially different in its features and manifestations to the person's psychological and biological attributes (Frankl, 2012). This element, which he called spirituality, is what enables the self to connect to its surroundings.

It is important to stress the essential human faculties of freedom, responsibility, and activity. This view, then, is far from seeing spirituality as mysticism or dogma. Understanding spirituality in this way—the value and meaning of its development in childhood, the setting in which pro-social behaviors and values are learned and a free, aware and responsible individual is shaped—seems completely without question.

There is no academic consensus on what exactly constitutes a religion. However, Bernard Lonergan (1988) sees it as a set of group experiences, meanings, convictions, beliefs, and expressive forms through which the group's members respond to the dialectics of self-transcendence and relationships with the divinity. In line with the American Psychology Association (APA), which explicitly includes religion in its definition of culture, we conceive of religions as cultural phenomena shaped by the means of production of their place of origin. Hence religion is seen as the interpretation of transcendent experience, since there can be no experience without interpretation.

As it has many cultural components, in a certain sense the interreligious relationship could be seen as an intercultural one. The religious experience does not take place in the abstract, but through "the cultural and psychic receptacles of each community and individual" (Melloni, 2003, p. 30).

Alfred Jeremias (cited in Coomaraswamy, 2001, p. 69) states that "cultural diversities are no other than the dialects of a single spiritual language"—here we distinguish between the two concepts. In our view, identification with a religious group does not necessarily presuppose religious experience. Also, there may be spiritual and religious experiences which do not involve identification with any institutionalised religion. We believe that it is highly important that educators should recognize these different possibilities since, as we have already remarked, certain facts with respect to formal religions should be seen in cultural rather than spiritual terms, and vice-versa.

What is beyond doubt, however, is that most people come into contact with spiritual practices and people in their daily lives when they talk to friends, family, and coworkers, or simply when they attend institutions such as schools. Given its relatively ubiquitous nature, everyone has an opinion on spirituality's place in society and, more specifically, on the forms it takes in religion or religions. Despite this, numerous studies show that many people lack basic knowledge of spirituality and the different world religions, even in their closest contexts. Preservice teachers are no exception to the rule (Marks, Binkley, & Daly, 2014).

SPIRITUALITY AND RELIGION IN THE LIFE OF THE CHILD

The benefits of proper spiritual development are important. In this respect, Claxton (2002) noted that spiritual development affords the person intense vitality, a feeling of belonging (in the sense of forming part of the world), composure in the face of uncertainty, and mental peace. Similarly, a study by Fraser and Grootenboer (2006) found that when the spiritual development of children was addressed in class (whether lay or religious), three outcomes could be identified:

1. The class took place in an atmosphere devoid of value judgments and criticisms;
2. Spiritual discourse was stimulated, with reflection on the other and the self on various levels; and
3. Deep meaning was given to those activities or events which could trigger transcendent experiences.

It should be stressed that spiritual development is not the same as the religious education, which can be found in many secular classrooms (Sternberg, 2003). At the same time, we do see a need for everyone to leave school with a functional understanding, at the very least, of a range of religions and their role in society, given the ubiquity of religion in our daily lives (Evans, 2007).

Seen from this perspective, the systemic value (Hellinger, 2008) of the heritage, models, and traditions of children's family religion, combined with its cultural and psycho-affective components, can afford a framework of security and affective attachment within which to grow in the first years of life, until freedom, responsibility, and the discovery of meaning show the young person which spiritual path they should follow. Thus, it is clearly valuable for education students to understand the importance of embracing the spiritual dimension in the classroom and favoring, as much as possible, its development from childhood onward. This is important from the conceptual perspective and from the perspective of its pedagogical approaches (Fraser & Grootenboer, 2006).

If on this point we return to one of our initial questions—has spirituality lost its value for our society?—we can answer, in the light of the above: not at all. In fact, both in its implications for physical, emotional, and affective health (Danso et al., 2003; Souza, 2009) and in its implications for social coexistence among citizens (Hart, 1997; Kerr & Cleaver, 2004; Watson, 2009), spirituality has a very high value.

Also, there is no place better than school—as a diverse, inclusive, and educational environment—to deal with spirituality and the religions. However, teachers are normally hesitant to take on these issues in class, for various reasons, many of which appear understandable; for example, their general lack of training in this area or their desire to avoid conflict with other members of the educational community, such as families. Certainly, the significance and meaning of religion for families has changed over time, although differently in each cultural context.

INTERCULTURAL AND INTERRELIGIOUS DIALOGUE IN EDUCATION

Cultural diversity, arising from migration and other globalizing trends, has produced fresh social landscapes in which new religious manifestations call on us to engage in interreligious dialogue. Interreligious and intercultural dialogue is the driving force needed to nurture peaceful coexistence in a pluralistic environment with diverse spiritual, religious, and cultural dimensions.

The European Union White Paper on Intercultural Dialogue (European Parliament and Council Decision 1983/2006/CE, 18 December 2006) defines dialogue as a process comprising an open and respectful exchange of views among individuals and groups of different ethnic, cultural, religious, and linguistic backgrounds and heritage, on the basis of mutual understanding and respect. The principles of intercultural and interreligious dialogue aim to:

- Develop the capacity to listen to others;
- Respect the diversity of beliefs;
- Identify common religious experiences;
- Be open to difference; and
- Give priority to ethics over dogmatism, emphasizing human rights and democracy and offering solutions to problems through a critical and participatory citizenship (Torradeflot, 2012).

Genuine interreligious dialogue is not limited to merely formal presentations of unreciprocated monologues, but involves an exchange which presupposes a willingness to rethink one's own ideas in the light of others—thus, opening the door to mutual enrichment and change among participants.

In some groups and communities, the natural desire for cohesion, preservation, and continuity is not offset by the desire for participation and coexistence; and if group members also believe that their own values are superior to those of the rest of society, and to other beliefs and convictions, and that their rights are the only valid ones, this can lead to a posture of closure, exclusion, and even hatred. Sometimes a closed stance of this kind can stem from a feeling of exclusion or persecution. Interreligious dialogue, in these cases, faces the challenge of finding ways to break down barriers.

All interreligious dialogue has three facets:

1. In a world where religious diversity is constantly growing and becoming more visible, the need arises to explore channels of communication between the various religious traditions. Only communication and trust can give rise to understanding, respect, and harmony among religious communities, on both local and global levels.
2. In a world that seeks peace, justice, and sustainability, religions have much to offer in terms of inspiring creative responses and motivating the will to change. Religious traditions share extremely important values which should be strengthened and put into practice through dialogue and cooperation.
3. In a world often marked by disorientation and even sadness, interreligious dialogue enables us—indirectly but inescapably—to explore in more depth each person's spiritual roots, their own traditions, and their personal process. Also, it contributes to self-enquiry and more genuine self-knowledge, while at the same time affording indisputable benefits through the knowledge of other religious traditions.

From the standpoint of these three facets, education in religious pluralism cannot be sterile. Education in pluralism will make peaceful coexistence and social cohesion possible, in addition to affording the creativity and imagination necessary to live in a meaningful way in an increasingly developed, knowledge-based society.

Two types of religious dialogue can be identified: the first is informal and the second is organized. The first is the living dialogue that arises in different situations of coexistence in plurality. Thus, people of diverse faiths and beliefs live and work together, sharing their lives and common spaces: shops, parks, school playgrounds, after-school activities, and the workplace canteen. The most important factor at this level is mutual respect, which may in some cases develop into friendship. These are invisible dialogues—unnoticed exchanges that are not consciously religious, but which strengthen human ties.

In contrast, organized dialogue arises on the initiative of civil society, the religious communities, and/or local government. From an ordinary citizen's standpoint, the aim is to attain broader and better mutual understanding through the organization of intercultural or social activities in their immediate context. Religious communities aim for interreligious meetings and dialogues to elucidate positive values and safeguard the shared traditions, interests, and priorities of the different faiths. Lastly, local government fosters interreligious initiatives for social cohesion by drawing in the religious communities with high cultural and religious diversity and potential for social conflict.

Schools are the most diverse habitats and are places where the vast majority of children live from their early years on. For this reason, they should be places where children and youth can share their own beliefs and be exposed to others with differing beliefs, both informally and in organized ways. In schools, students not only experience the world, but also have support for understanding it, analyzing it critically and reflectively, and adopting a posture toward the world and how to care for it.

There certainly does not exist a single practice or means of helping teachers learn how to integrate interreligious dialogue and religious issues into their study programs. However, a good starting point for laying the foundations is in teacher training. This is evident as future educators can begin to learn about the place and meaning of religions in education (Tanneabum, 2018).

LEARNING ENVIRONMENTS FOR SPIRITUAL DEVELOPMENT

The foundations of an environment favoring spiritual development are common and transferable to all educational levels. These foundations comprise a series of cognitive, affective, and emotional components that foster the development of spiritual awareness. According to Eisner (1995, p. 765), the cognitive dimension of learning environments for spiritual development "make it possible for students to think imaginatively about problems which concern them, explore issues which do not have easy or obvious answers, broach topics which express their own ideas."

Spirituality cannot be understood apart from its association with emotion. Feelings of compassion, disconcertment, or acceptance necessarily form part of the relationship with the other and with oneself, which is typical of spirituality. Its development thus calls for learning situations in which sensations and feelings can arise and be shaped (Hyde, 2006). A ludic educational atmosphere is ideal for enabling feelings to surface in a nonthreatening climate in which students can experience, experiment, describe, and think about them. On the other hand, the cognitive and affective elements basically represent reactions to stimuli presented in class.

The spiritual dimension thus emerges as a process of self-reflection in which students express which aspects of self-transformation have taken place during the course of the activity (Souza, 2003; 2004). Buchanan and Hyde (2008, p. 39) illustrate how these elements should be integrated: "a student can learn about the causes of poverty in the third world (cognitive). On the basis of this analysis s/he can understand the suffering of people who undergo hunger due to poverty (affective). A deep understanding of this poverty-based suffering can be a transformative experience in which the student asks her/himself what s/he can do (behavioural) to help alleviate poverty in the third world."

TEACHER EDUCATION FOR FOSTERING INTERRELIGIOUS DIALOGUE IN CLASS

The American Psychological Association (APA) advocates developing programs to prepare students for cultural and religious diversity. In addition, directives for convergence from the United Nations, the United Nations Educational, Scientific and Cultural Organisation (UNESCO), and the Council of Europe stipulate that education should respect the right to freedom of thought, conscience, and religion, and that all discrimination based on belief should be eradicated, as this represents an offence to human dignity and threatens peaceful coexistence.

One pedagogical approach to eradicating such discrimination is to recognize, discuss, and deconstruct the problem of perceptions of otherness, which are deeply rooted and therefore embedded, silent, and invisible. The long-established tendency to mix and simplify ethnic, national, linguistic, religious, and phenotypical differences—complex, diverse, and never completely discrete and dichotomous—into black-and-white, us-and-them distinctions still contributes to "essentializing" and overrepresenting the historical "other."

Understanding the diversity and the depth of religions and traditional wisdom affords personal enrichment and mutual recognition, favoring peaceful coexistence and respect, and helping to prevent fundamentalist postures. In our view, it is necessary to offer basic training in the knowledge of religious diversity and nonreligious beliefs, including atheism, agnosticism, and indifference. Mental rigidity is linked to stereotypes, prejudices, and discrimination on cultural and religious grounds.

The development of competencies for awareness of cultural and religious diversity, then, can be a starting point for overcoming these discriminatory tendencies. Also needed are tools for a culture of peace, and an intercultural education with a sound pedagogical grounding in ethics and values, ranging from hospitality and mutual recognition to caring for others and the inescapable responsibility of solidarity toward all people.

At present there is a need for a new interreligious sensibility, combined with the development of an intrinsic human dimension, the spiritual dimension inherent in all human beings resulting from the experience of religious diversity as an opportunity for mutual enrichment and a renewed and deepened consciousness. Some of the objectives which should be present in programs for promoting interreligious dialogue are:

- Promoting relationships between believers from the different religions present in the school.
- Favoring mutual knowledge, understanding, respect, and tolerance between believers from different religious traditions.
- Exploring shared ethics.
- Working together to promote social coherence and peaceful coexistence; to combat ignorance, fear, and hatred between people of different religious traditions and between these and nonreligious people; to prevent and deconstruct prejudices and stereotypes among believers; to heal the pain and wounds caused by the intolerance embedded in believers' collective memory; and to attempt to build new memories arising from shared experiences of peace and dialogue.
- To be a public voice and, when appropriate, a common voice for the religious communities; to make declarations on relevant topics and challenges as they arise.
- To cultivate friendship between people of diverse faiths and convictions.
- To engage and encourage the participation of local religious communities in the civic life of the school.
- To bring together local religious communities and the school to discuss subjects of mutual interest.
- To organize and carry out projects and activities fostering interreligious education.

- To provide opportunities for students to learn the religious rites, ceremonies, and practices of the different religions.
- To facilitate dialogue and more in-depth knowledge of the various spiritual traditions through introduction and recognition of, and respect for, the diversity of spiritual models and practices.
- To offer tools to the religious communities for discussing and acting jointly on social topics, particularly those involving solidarity and nondiscrimination.
- To exchange the artistic heritage of all the traditions and to design and share joint artistic activities demonstrating harmony and coexistence among traditions.

Religion and spirituality are dimensions that affect children's education, as we remarked at the beginning of this chapter. This means that teachers at all levels, including early childhood teachers, need to understand and embrace these topics in their professional practice. Even though the highly abstract and complex nature of spirituality means that children in preschool will rarely use reasoning relating to the divine, unlike students at higher levels (Wenger, 2001), it is necessary for teachers to have at least some training in this area.

The hope is that teachers will be able to respond to their students' ideas and explanations, whatever the nature of their reasoning, because it is exactly at this stage when emotional and spiritual development begin to give rise to the formation of judgment. In some studies, for example, it has been found that young children from the least religious families tend to give more factual explanations than those from more religious families. Given their limited powers of abstraction, these children depend largely on information provided by adults (Sharon & Woolley, 2004).

In addition, promoting intercultural and interreligious dialogue in education requires training which takes teachers further afield than just the knowledge of diversity, involving the professional and personal empowerment of teachers. For this empowerment, three key areas are paramount:

- The *area of identity*: the teacher as a reflective practitioner when dealing with religious diversity and prejudices/stereotyping
- The *pedagogical area*: the teacher as facilitator of interreligious dialogue in the classroom
- The *community area*: the teacher as facilitator of the relationships between school, family and community

The Reflective Teacher: An Opportunity for Preservice Teacher Education Programs

Among the possibilities for articulating spaces in which trainee teachers can develop a "culturally responsive pedagogy" featuring religion as a factor for discussion and analysis, critical thinking is worth special mention. The development of reflective and critical professional identities in our field should be linked to an understanding of the commitment to change and the transformation of the social and educational context from the standpoint of inclusion; this is an essential starting point for apprehending how religion can adapt and conform to the ideas of interculturality and social cohesion.

Becoming a reflective and critical professional means analyzing, questioning, and redefining one's own role as a teacher. Stenhouse (1985), advocate of the teacher as researcher, argued that educational change and development takes place through teachers' reflective skills. Critical and reflective skills enable teachers to assess and learn about their practice and reconstruct the complexity of their own teaching experience in the interreligious situation of the school and their classrooms. Dialogue, communication, working together, and discussion among professionals are approaches for training and transforming the person and educational practice.

This reflective and critical professional identity should complement the different identities each person has, such as religious identity. Belonging to a religious group is understood here as a social or collective dimension of identity, similar to gender or ethnicity. Identity offers a form of belonging that is a source of meaning, security, and community, increasingly necessary in the contemporary world. Judicious management of these diverse identity models and of relationships with those who are different is a key factor to take into account in interreligious dialogue and for eradicating the hegemonic attitudes of one religion toward another or others, which can lead to discrimination.

When faced with discrimination on religious grounds, developing the skills of self-awareness and self-criticism enables us to overcome the fears and defensive attitudes that are often behind all types of discrimination and social exclusion, and to avoid stereotyping. Pedagogical skills for eliminating such discrimination are oriented toward critical awareness of negative, simplistic, or even false "information" that does not favor mutual understanding but feeds hatred and prejudices. Thus, it is necessary to avoid absolute ideas on God or the ultimate reality, and accept that others have different ideas.

In fact, the purpose is to explicitly work with the attitudes of future teachers to eradicate stereotyping and discriminatory attitudes. One approach to this type of training is based on debate and reflection on concepts such as ethnocentricity, the right to difference, plurality and pluralism, ethnicity, nationality, nationalism, race, racism, antiracism, colonialism, and so on.

This debate should lead the preservice teacher to identify a particular situation of conflict experienced in her or his practice; or conversely, a lived experience can give rise to a debate on the concepts mentioned, including knowledge of religious traditions.

This debate enables an analysis of the teacher's ego and thus can begin to make explicit the teacher's attitudes, prejudices, stereotypes, and implicit theories and question these. Various questions can help the preservice teacher in this exploration, such as: How did I feel in this situation of interreligious conflict in the classroom? Can I give a name to this feeling? Why did I feel that way? What aspects of my person is it calling into question? What influence does my family have in the conflict I experienced? How can I work on this influence? Do my family and my social environment condition me? What can I do about this?

These initial steps in training the preservice teacher can prompt a debate on wearing religious symbols in schools. Although presumably in early childhood this situation is not so visible and obvious, at the same time serious, dispassionate debate is still necessary if we are to avert ethnic and religious prejudices around the use of religious symbols in schools. We see schools as public places free of such symbols, but at the same time accepting the individual freedom to wear them privately (the hijab, the cross, etc.). In educational spheres, in particular in the school as a public arena, it is recommended to act in favor of nonconfessionality, secularism, and religious plurality.

Despite apparent changes in the public spheres of western societies, the argument of impartiality is still the most common response to unfamiliar cultural and religious precepts. This suggests that there is a certain contradiction in this precept, which, while affirming the state's neutrality in matters of faith, at the same time actively limits the religious communities' aspirations to public presence, especially for those not sharing the state's own cultural ethos.

In view of these new religious presences, it may be argued that we are now living in a plural society, where in the west the Christian Church is no longer the sole model in the market of religious values. However, in many cases recognition of religious pluralism is more formal than real, since a more typical approach to pluralism is simple description of the range of different religious models. Thus, the preservice teacher and preservice teacher education programs should offer ways to recognize the contributions of the different religions to the shaping of our society as a plural reality.

PROMOTING INTERRELIGIOUS DIALOGUE IN EARLY CHILDHOOD

Education should promote respect, understanding, tolerance, and dialogue among different religions and cultures. It should have an increasingly intercultural character in order to teach children about culture in its broadest aspects (languages, civilizations, traditions, art, religions, beliefs, customs, etc.). For this reason, educators in this area should seek to enhance coexistence through knowledge of the other, thereby favoring understanding between cultures and dialogue between religions.

While it is true that knowledge of the other does not in itself guarantee dialogue, it is an essential requisite for such dialogue. If this knowledge is offered with the necessary empathy and in a critical spirit, it will have all the necessary ingredients for fostering a culture of dialogue that will make living together and exchanging cultures possible.

Furthermore, teachers may fear creating problems if they talk about and work on religions with their students. However, in reality, the vast majority of their concerns can be addressed if their training programs help them understand their rights and the difference between indoctrination and simple exposition to diverse views. In other words, teachers should be able to discuss the topic of religion objectively.

Thus, the preservice teacher and preservice teacher education programs should ensure that they nurture a school environment promoting inclusive education, where children can discuss the placing of sites of worship and the occupation of communal space. While it is true that there is no single way of teaching how interreligious dialogue should be fostered, it is essential that we introduce new practical methods equipping teachers for their work in the classroom. Child educators should be exposed to different teaching approaches for working with spirituality, religions, and interreligious dialogue, providing them with situations such as case studies, ethical dilemmas, and simulations.

In early childhood classrooms, many teaching approaches traditionally used for teaching values and interculturality can also be adopted. This is vital for assimilating the theoretical contents of history and religion and influencing the pedagogical decisions taken in the classroom. It is not enough for teachers to be exposed more broadly to the religions; they also should become aware of their roles and responsibilities toward these topics. They need to personally experience how religions are present and should be embraced in the classroom and its management.

In addition to this, training programs should follow these guidelines:

- Avoid cultural essentialism and exclusive religious dogmatism
- Uphold the higher good of the child

- Recognize and act consistently with the main principles underpinning educational practice and peaceful coexistence
- Take care when setting regulations affecting basic rights and prevailing legislation
- See the school as an area where a common ethic is taught, learned and practiced

Promoting intercultural dialogue entails reconsidering justice as a guiding principle of social relations. Justice both makes and recognizes demands. From the *a priori* standpoint of respect for all religious identities without proselytizing, the mainstays of interreligious dialogue are receptive listening and honest testimony. For this reason, it can be one of our most useful tools for easing situations of conflict and facilitating reconciliation, since religious traditions can help their followers move beyond narrow self-interest toward a greater collective good. This religious dimension can contribute to peace and social cohesion.

To this end, teacher education programmes should (1) foster the principles of dialogue; (2) foster the knowledge of different religious traditions; and (3) foster shared values that can strengthen social cohesion. These principles are discussed below.

Fostering the principles of dialogue. The principles of interreligious dialogue in preservice teacher education programs should aim to develop the ability to listen and to promote knowledge of the other, respect for diversity of beliefs, identification of common religious experiences, openness to differences, and prioritizing of ethics over dogma (the precedence of human rights and democracy in seeking solutions to problems with a critical and participatory citizenry).

This entails a type of education that also addresses teachers' attitudes, as we saw in the previous section. Strategies for cooperation and participation are good for developing competencies in interreligious dialogue, since they bring into play respect for others and the capacity to listen, among other strengths. Preservice teachers, through the conflict situation they have experienced in class, learn to put themselves in the place of the other, open themselves to difference, and understand the other. Depending on what situations they have encountered, a particular case may then be able to prompt debate on the priority of ethics over dogma.

Fostering knowledge of religious traditions. Religious culture is knowing the diversity and depth of religious traditions and knowledge (Estivalèzes, 2017; Green et al., 2018). We must have mutual understanding by facilitating coexistence and respect, and averting fundamentalist attitudes. We should go beyond the secularization of societies marked by their deep ignorance of religions. This lack of knowledge leads to an illiteracy around the meanings of many of our own traditional celebrations or typical words in our own vocabulary.

Preservice teacher training programs should offer a basic education in the knowledge of religious diversity—not only because this represents a valuable cultural, ethical, and spiritual heritage, but because society needs to learn from its legacy of wisdom in order to find its way in the present and progress toward a more human, peaceful, equitable, and sustainable future. Likewise, training programs should also afford information and education on the religious diversity found in our streets and classrooms. This should be done through acceding to and visiting places of worship, which function as identity models, meeting points, places of refuge and, above all, sites of spiritual experience, both personal and communitarian.

It is important that this basic education should be solidly grounded, since in the educational field it is common to offer partial and/or erroneous religious information, generalizations, stereotypes, and lack of rigor in presentations and use of texts and images from religious cultures other than the hegemonic ones. To this end, it is important to develop teachers' critical capacity when revising curricula and teaching texts.

There is a clear and urgent need to offer both publishers and teachers resources that give access to rigorous information on religious traditions, which would enable them to discuss these in class from the standpoint of proportional parity and nondiscrimination. Thus, we should create materials on cultural and religious diversity that favor plurality, recognition of the other, and empathy.

Education in the knowledge of religious diversity is vital in our society. We should be particularly careful that curricula should not incite hatred or fear toward any religion or nonreligious philosophy, or obstruct the will to work on spiritual sensibility and intelligence. Furthering the right to religious freedom has much to do with knowledge of religious diversity in one's own setting and with the recognition of this diversity as a positive thing. Evaluating the legacy of pluralism educationally, culturally, and religiously—not as an obstacle, but as a specific resource—will bring to light its potential for building solid bridges between cultures.

The purpose of education in interreligious sensibility is not only to encourage dialogue and understanding in coexistence of different religious faiths. The purpose is to also nurture sensitivity toward the cultivation of each person's spiritual roots, explicitly reclaiming spiritual sensibility as a positive value in promoting self-exploration and the quest for meaning.

Fostering shared values and strengthening social cohesion. The preservice teacher and preservice teacher education programs should opt for a type of intercultural education with a sound pedagogical grounding in values education; more specifically, in a basic set of powerful values ranging from hospitality and mutual recognition to consideration for others and the inescapable responsible of solidarity toward all human beings. There is an urgent need for a radical, ethical education capable of overcoming all types of egoism, and thereby making an enriching intercultural coexistence possible.

This commitment to fostering shared values leads us to the study of ethics, and means that the teacher must be conversant with existing resources for evidencing and cultivating the common base of values among religious traditions and nonreligious beliefs and for encouraging respect toward differences, especially through the integration of religious culture into normal, everyday life. This means favoring an attitude of closeness to others, involving tolerance, hospitality, mutual esteem, integration, and promotion of the culture of peace.

Preservice teacher education programs have the opportunity to strengthen social cohesion through new and sustainable approaches that include religious diversity. Thus, we advocate embracing religious issues as a means of socially integrating immigrant groups, since it is a key way of helping migrants maintain ties with their origins while at the same time encouraging the rooting of identity in the host country.

When defining an educational model for boosting religious diversity, the preservice teacher should opt for an education in values linked to social cohesion and promoting:

- Manifestations of religious diversity in schools;
- Bringing children into contact with different values and perspectives on the world to shape their individual identities; and
- Incorporating the religious dimension in a way that boosts understanding, peaceful coexistence, inclusion, and participation, bearing in mind the principles of tolerance, reciprocity, and civic thinking.

FAMILY, COMMUNITY, AND RELIGION IN EARLY CHILDHOOD

Early childhood daily shares two microcontexts: the family and the school. Typically, children move from the family to the school and back again. These two settings have common objectives, such as the proper upbringing of children and support and guidance for their development in all aspects: emotional, personal, cognitive, affective, and relational.

Likewise, a main function of both contexts is the care and protection of the child. Although both school and family share this purpose, the organization of space and time, the people involved, and the activities undertaken are different. The specific contrast we would like to highlight here, in relation to interreligious competencies, is not only in the type of language used in the two settings, but also the actual language spoken.

The family language may differ from that of the school, as it does in many societies, while at the same time the school's language tends to be much more decontextualized, making references to objects and phenomena that are not present in the classroom. Thus, when children start in early years education, they face an environment very different from that of their families, although family and school are the main socializing settings of childhood. This means that there is an *a priori* discontinuity between school and family.

School and Family

Bronfenbrenner (1979) found that children's participation in a range of different contexts aids their development. From this point of view, the discontinuity between school and family has positive effects on children's development, since each setting affords different types of learning experiences. However, this discontinuity can also be negative if the approach is unilateral, that is, from the hegemonic perspective of a dominant mainstream culture.

This dominant discourse is built on the assumption that school and family belong to the same culture, sharing their culture's ideal goals in the areas of values, religious beliefs, and behavior. Thus, from the standpoint of continuity between the two settings, children and families who do not share this culture can be plunged into an acute contradiction between what happens at school and what happens at home, thus hindering their development and adaptation to schooling. This situation is especially harmful in early childhood, since children at this age feel these discrepancies particularly sharply. This is why, for this age group, family and school should attempt to be consistent with each other in order to reduce the discontinuity.

In an intercultural and interreligious society, schools and their teachers face the significant challenge of seeking convergent aspects of families' religions and beliefs in order to overcome the contradictions between the two settings. These aspects are found, among other things, in autonomy, dialogue, respect for otherness, and the common values held by religions, such as peace.

It is not a question of imposing any particular moral code or belief, or even that these should be the same, but of creating a type of school that is open to religious diversity and to interreligious dialogue, where each member of the community (family, teachers, students) feels at home. This is not an easy task, given that the concepts of public and private space are embodied in the family-school relationship.

The family signifies private space: an intimate area that has been socially legitimized by culture and religion, a system of values, a specific form of spirituality which transmits a model for life (acceptable behavior, values, management of emotions, attitudes toward life events, etc.) and which in general has been approved by the rest of society (Prats, 2012). School in the early childhood years represents the public space that will confirm to the family (or not) the life model it is building, including the upbringing of children.

If the school is not open to religious diversity and interreligious dialogue, it will demand that the family adapt to the school setting; in other words, that the family should revise its function in the area of religion. If the public institution is more open, however, it is less likely that the family will demand continuity from it in terms of religious beliefs, cultural customs, and relational rules. If the school, as a public space, is organized as an open system that accepts religious diversity, then it can work through interreligious dialogue to avoid conflicts with families over their religion and to eradicate religious discrimination and fundamentalist attitudes.

School and Community

School should become the public sphere where religious differences are encountered, since it is the only institution compelled to group together all children without any form of discrimination. For some children, school is the only place where they can live alongside "different others."

We know that a large number of families, particularly those who feel that they are in a minority due to their religious beliefs (though not only these), perform all of their activities within their religious communities. If this is a source of security on the one hand, on the other it involves isolation from the rest of society. Thus, schools in any neighborhood of a city or town must offer a secular atmosphere to all children and their families. This is because schools, particularly state schools, constitute a formal setting with religious diversity.

The school provides a first experience of secularism in the daily aspects of children's lives and its informal areas, such as the playground. One example of this can be found in the different menus offered to families, respecting the rules of different religious traditions. But this should go further, because it is not enough to just provide these menus, or an institutionalized "Religions Day," or a school festival of secular rituals. It is a question, of fostering a climate of dialogue that favors participation and collaboration between the two settings. Early childhood education is the period of schooling where this joint work should be stressed most, for two main reasons:

1. This initial relationship will give form to all subsequent collaborations for the rest of the child's time in school. A constructive connection between family and teachers at the outset favors the maintenance of this positive relationship in the coming years.
2. Early childhood schools tend to be children's first contact outside the home at times when the family is not present. For this reason, strong

relational ties should be created in order to facilitate the transition from the private sphere to the public, avoiding any fear or rejection of school could impact the child's later schooling.

Participating in various mutual awareness activities helps families and their children discover the different other. For example, sharing typical food between families of different origins and belief systems, or some type of performance piece by the families on their religion or religious culture, provides opportunities to increase mutual knowledge.

These spaces for mutual awareness foster the identity of each person and each group of different cultural and religious origins, and bring children's identities into a relationship with those of others. They are spaces of mutual respect, which in some cases can encourage the first ties of friendship, and they strengthen human relationships by promoting invisible dialogues that may pass unnoticed by the very people who are experiencing them and who are not, in fact, consciously religious. This is informal interreligious dialogue.

Promoting a climate of dialogue means that the teacher has dialogic and communicative competencies, capacity for empathy, and a knowledge of the family roles and functions prescribed by religious traditions. In most of these, women have secondary status, below that of men, in their opinions, decisions, and attributions. The preservice teacher should take these situations into account and can serve as a model for the empowerment of women, in this case the mothers who are their contacts in the families. It is in early childhood that gender roles and their attendant stereotypes are forged, and for this reason it is also necessary to promote dignity, gender equality, and justice in the various religious and spiritual traditions and in interreligious initiatives.

The preservice teacher and preservice teacher education programs should promote gender equality and respect for democratic freedoms within religious traditions and interreligious dialogue. The aim is to construct and exemplify values, and offer an alternative to the relationships of domination stemming from patriarchy, expressed in specific relations between men and women, but also in the alienation of all those who are seen as different. Furthermore, we should develop a form of education which balances the masculine and feminine aspects of each person, moving beyond gender roles and boosting critical awareness.

Working in Networks

Boosting working in networks is one of the objectives schools should have. The school is the ideal place for creating links with different religious and belief-based organizations. In this way the school represents a mesosystem that supports mutual recognition between different beliefs and organizations. At the preschool stage, specific activities can be undertaken to develop these relationships. One of the most utilized of these is school visits from members of different religious communities or, alternatively, children's visits to these communities or to social organizations working on religious diversity.

Working in networks can enable schools to come into contact with different structures and systems in the community, such as the neighborhood and the city. In addition, different educational networks operating in the area at the local, regional, national, or even international level can become relevant systems of support.

In these structures, systems, and networks, the school encounters various actors such as nongovernmental organizations, civil associations, religious communities, political parties, and private individuals. All of these should be committed to democratic management of cultural and religious diversity. The school cannot remain isolated from other educational actors in its environment. Dialogue with all active agents in the area (religious communities, local residents, businesses, users of its facilities, etc.) is fundamental.

Respecting the principles of neutrality and impartiality, it is necessary to engage different religious traditions in civil society in general, in order to encourage initiatives that will be increasingly open to a positive and inclusive view of otherness from the standpoint of respect and tolerance. Only the guarantee of rights and mutual respect can enable joint work between the administration and religious communities in order to overcome the idea that diversity is an anomaly. This should also take into account the complexity of the state and private systems, and problems in places with interreligious conflicts.

Working in networks boosts interreligious dialogue. This dialogue can take place around three key areas:

1. The first area stems from civil society initiatives; that is, from groups of people normally of different religious and/or spiritual traditions. The purpose of these networks is to attain better understanding and mutual knowledge, which can build greater social cohesion. To this end, they tend to organize intercultural or social activities in their areas, open to the whole community.
2. A second area of dialogue is provided by different religious communities, particularly when problems of racism or xenophobia arise. These links stem from a specific community or from various communities with a common objective. The basis of the networking is dialogue between religious communities and/or their representatives in order to seek positive values shared by all religions and to safeguard the common interests and priorities of the religious communities.

3. The third area is part of government policies at all levels, but mainly municipal administration, since this is the closest to citizens. These initiatives are therefore the actions of politicians, but also of professional administrators, aiming to create interreligious initiatives. The purpose of these initiatives is to guarantee peace and social cohesion. They tend to be carried out in neighborhoods and cities with wide cultural and religious diversity and potential for social conflict.

The first and second areas are made up of groups which we could call interreligious groups, organized according to their purpose: mutual recognition, study and research, deepening knowledge and spiritual exchange, social cohesion and mediation, and institutional representation (Torradeflot, 2012).

Interreligious groups for mutual recognition seek mutual understanding through interpersonal relations and dialogue aimed at discovering the other's identity. The objective is to overcome the mistrust that normally exists between people of different religious affiliations, even the hostility normally embodied in extremist groups.

Beginning to trust the different other can be the starting point of friendship but, essentially, it allows the various members of the group to relate to each other in a climate of confidence. Thus, these are groups open to all, regardless of their religion or beliefs. They are organized through regular face-to-face meetings, combined with shared meals and interreligious events that enable them to broaden their bases.

Interreligious groups for study and research operate in the area of academic dialogue, since they include experts, academics, and university students, along with believers from different traditions. Members exchange and discuss the theological-philosophical bases of their different traditions. The aim is to reach a shared understanding of the way in which each religious tradition approaches reality. A topic of debate is normally proposed (e.g., peace, the role of women in religions, immigration). The group's analysis is disseminated through different media to help eliminate prejudices and false ideas through an interreligious platform. This kind of group offers access to public debate.

Interreligious groups for spiritual dialogue, also called spiritual deepening or exchange, are the most intense and conciliatory. They can provide particularly deep experiences for their participants and inspiration for other forms of dialogue (Panikkar, 2005). The purpose of this type of group is for believers, spiritual people, and mystics to encounter each other in order to set out their spiritual lives and religious practices. The main interest is not in debate, unlike the study group. These dialogues are organized around practices of meditation or group silence, and peer teaching.

Interreligious groups for social cohesion and mediation arise in towns and neighborhoods with wide diversity and a certain amount of interreligious conflict. Thus, these groups are made up of members of civil organizations, social service workers, and education and health professionals. They seek to promote social cohesion and peaceful coexistence, work toward peace and against discrimination, and defend rights and disadvantaged groups.

Lastly, interreligious groups for institutional representation are composed of the authorities within different religious communities who act as spokespeople. These figures organize themselves into councils, forums, or assemblies aimed at achieving a joint voice and lead dialogue in their respective faith communities. They are normally groups for negotiating with government agencies.

Clearly, such networking will also contribute to curricular pluralism, through approaches aimed at boosting education and knowledge. Also, the training of the leaders should also be aimed at promoting exchanges between public institutions and different programs.

CONCLUSIONS

Teachers are models to follow for children and, therefore, teacher education is essential for this stage of life, if we take into consideration the nature of the topic we are discussing here. The education sciences promote the training of professionals oriented toward decision-making, and to this end the inclusion of pluricultural perspectives is vital. The hope is that discussions of the various religious practices will take place in teacher education, since students need to learn about culture in its broadest and most secular sense. To address questions on the role played by spirituality and religion in early childhood, and specifically in preservice teacher education programs, we should therefore respond on the basis of four main areas, shown in figure 4.1.

The first area is the in-depth grasp of spirituality and religion: understanding spirituality, and the value and the meaning of its development in early childhood, as a sphere where prosocial behavior and values and the free, self-aware, responsible person are shaped. Spiritual development does not involve religious instruction, although it is necessary for citizens to have, at the very least, a functional understanding of various religions and their role in society. The presence of different religions in the same social context requires a new public culture in the realm of religious issues.

Preservice teacher training programs should offer a basic education in the knowledge of religious diversity, not only because it is a valuable cultural, ethical, and spiritual heritage, but also because society needs to learn from its legacy and wisdom in order to find its way in the present and progress toward a more human, peaceful, equitable, and sustainable future. Thus, we advocate embracing religious issues as a means of socially integrating immigrant groups, since it is a key way of helping migrants to maintain ties with their

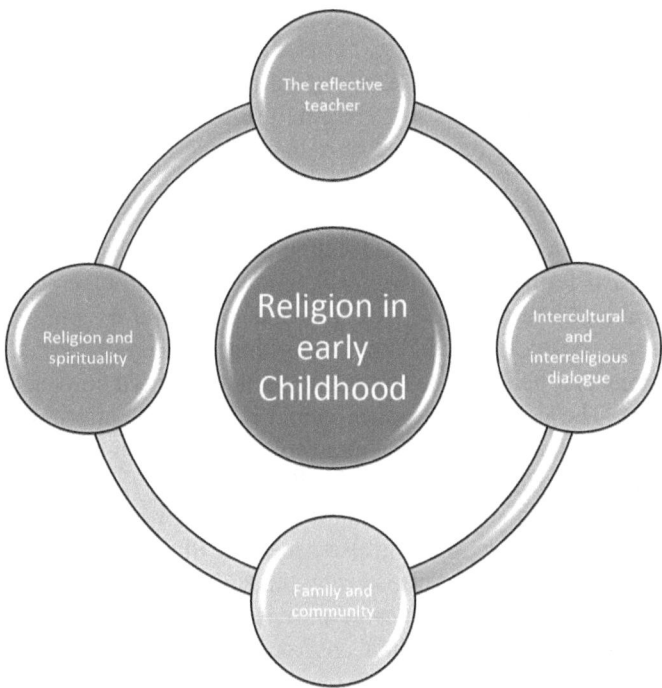

Figure 4.1. Main areas of professional and personal empowerment in preservice teacher training programs. *Source:* Developed by the authors.

origins, while at the same time encouraging the rooting of identity in the host country.

The second area is intercultural and interreligious dialogue. Cultural diversity, an outcome of migration and other globalizing factors, creates fresh social landscapes in which new religious manifestations prompt us to engage in interreligious dialogue. Interreligious and intercultural dialogue is the driving force needed to promote peaceful coexistence in a plural environment with a diversity of spiritual, religious, and cultural dimensions.

The principles of interreligious dialogue in preservice teacher education programs should aim to develop the ability to listen, knowledge of the other, respect for diversity of beliefs, identification of common religious experiences, openness to differences, and prioritizing ethics over dogma (the precedence of human rights and democracy in seeking solutions to problems with a critical and participatory citizenry).

The third area is based on the teacher's reflective role. Critical and reflective skills enable preservice teachers to foster, assess, and learn from their own practice and to reconstruct the complexity of their teaching experience in the interreligious context of the school and their own classrooms. Dialogue, communication, collaboration, and discussion among professionals are strategies not only for training, but also for transforming those involved and their educational practices. Developing the capacity for self-awareness and self-criticism enables us to overcome the fears and defensive attitudes that often lie behind all types of discrimination and social exclusion, and to avoid stereotyping.

Lastly, the fourth area is consideration of the community and family dimension in preservice teacher education programs. Young children daily move back and forth between two settings: the family and the school. In an intercultural and interreligious society, the school—and therefore its teachers—face the considerable challenge of seeking convergent aspects in families' religions and beliefs order to overcome the contradictions between the two settings. The preservice teacher should take this situation into account and can serve as a model for the empowerment of women—in this case, the mothers who are their contacts in the families.

It is in early childhood that gender roles and their attendant stereotypes are forged, and for this reason it is also necessary to promote dignity, gender equality, and justice in the various religious and spiritual traditions and in interreligious initiatives. At the same time, schools cannot remain isolated; dialogue with other actors in their environments is essential, for example with religious communities.

REFERENCES

Bronfenbrenner, U. (1979). *The ecology of human development: Experiments by nature and design*. Cambridge, MA: Harvard University Press.

Buchanan, M., & Hyde, B. (2008). Learning beyond the surface: Engaging the cognitive, affective and spirituality within the curriculum. *International Journal of Children's Spirituality*, *13*(4), 309–320.

Casal, J., Garcia, M., & Merino, R. (2007). Los sistemas educativos comprensivos ante las vías y los itinerarios formativos. *Revista de Educación*, *342*, 213–237.

Claxton, G. (2002). Mind expanding: Scientific and spiritual foundations for the schools we need [Paper presentation]. Graduate School of Education Public Lectures. Bristol, UK: University of Bristol.

Coomaraswamy, A. K. (2001). *El vedama y la tradición occidental*. Madrid: Siruela.

Danso, C., Greaves, H., Howell, S., Ryan, M., Sinclair, R., & Tunnard, J. (2003). *The involvement of children and young people in promoting change and enhancing the quality of social care: a research review*. London, UK: National Children's Bureau.

Eisner, E. (1995). Standards for American schools: Help or hindrance? *Phi Delta Kappan*, *76*(10), 765–769.

Estivalèzes, M. (2017). The professional stance of ethics and religious culture teachers in Québec. *British Journal of Religious Education*, *39*(1), 55–74. https://doi.org/10.1080/01416200.2015.1128339

Evans, M. P. (2007). Learning to teach about religion in public schools: Perspectives and experiences of student teachers in the Program for Religion and Secondary Education at Harvard Divinity School. *Religion and Education*, *34*(3), 19–47.

Frankl, V. (2012). *La presencia ignorada de Dios*. Barcelona: Herder.

Fraser, D., & Grootenboer, P. (2006). Nurturing spirituality in secular classrooms. *International Journal of Children's Spirituality*, *9*(3), 307–320.
Green, A. R., Tulissi, A., Erais, S., Cairns, S. L., & Bruckner, D. (2018). Building an inclusive campus: Developing students' intercultural competencies through an interreligious and intercultural diversity program. *Canadian Journal of Higher Education*, *48*(3), 43–64.
Hart, R. (1997). *Children's participation: The theory and practice of involving young citizens in community development and environmental Care*. New York: UNICEF.
Hellinger, B. (2008). *Órdenes del amor*. Barcelona: Herder.
Hyde, B. (2006). Nurturing the spirit in primary religious education classrooms. In M. Souza, G. Durka, K. Engebretson, R. Jackson, & A. McGrady (Eds.), *International Handbook of the religious, moral and spiritual dimension in education* (pp. 1179–1192). Dordrecht, The Netherlands: Springer.
Kerr, D., & Cleaver, E. (2004). *Citizenship education longitudinal study: Literature review— citizenship education one year on—what does it mean? Emerging definitions and approaches in the first year of national curriculum citizenship in England*. Nottingham, UK: DfES publications.
Lonergan, B. (1988). *Religión: Método en teología*. Salamanca: Sígueme.
Marks, M. J., Binkley, R., & Daly, J. K. (2014). Preservice teachers and religion: Serious gaps in religious knowledge and the First Amendment. *The Social Studies*, *105*(5), 245–256.
McInerney, P. (2004). *Making hope practical: School reform for social justice*. Mawson Lake, Australia: Centre for Research in Education, Equity and Work.
Melloni, J. (2003). Accesos a la interioridad. *Sal Terrae: Revista de Teología Pastoral*, *91*(1063), 33–42.
Panikkar, R. (2005). *De la mística: Experiencia plena de la vida*. Barcelona: Herder.
Prats, E. (2012). El entorno de la escuela como facilitador de una pedagogía inclusiva en materia religiosa. In J. L. Álvarez & M. À. Essomba (Eds.), *Dioses en las aulas. Educación y diálogo interreligioso* (pp. 255–276). Barcelona: Graó.
Sharon, T., & Woolley, J. D. (2004). Do monsters dream? Young children's understanding of the fantasy/reality distinction. *British Journal of Developmental Psychology*, *22*, 293–310.
Souza, M. (2003). Contemporary influences on the spirituality of young people: Implications for education. *International Journal of Children's Spirituality*, *8*(3), 269–279.
Souza, M. (2004). Teaching effective learning in religious education: A discussion of the perceiving, thinking, feeling and intuitive elements in the learning process. *Journal of Religious Education*, *52*(3), 22–30.
Souza, M. (2009). Spirituality and well-being. *International Journal of Children's Spirituality*, *14*(3), 181–184.
Sternberg, R. J. (2003). *Wisdom, intelligence, and creativity synthesize*. New York: Cambridge University Press.
Stenhouse, L. (1985) Investigación y desarrollo del curriculum. Madrid: Morata, pp. 194 -221.
Tanneabum, R. P. (2018). Teaching about religion within early childhood and elementary social studies: Exploring how preservice teachers perceive their rights and responsibilities as educators. *Journal of Social Studies Education Research*, *9*(4), 30–48.
Torradeflot, F. (2012). *Catalunya i el diàleg interreligiós. Aportacions innovadores al diàleg interreligiós des dels valors de les Nacions Unides*. Barcelona: Associació UNESCO per al diàleg interreligiós.
United Nations General Assembly. (1959, November 20). Declaration of the Rights of the Child. A/RES/1386(XIV). https://www.refworld.org/docid/3ae6b38e3.html
Watson, J. (2009). Preparing spirituality for citizenship. *International Journal of Children's Spirituality*, *8*(1), 9–24.
Welbourne, L. (2000). Religious education and outcomes-based curriculum. *Journal of Religious Education*, *48*, 1–11.
Wenger, J. L. (2001). Children's theories of God: Explanations for difficult-to-explain phenomena. *Journal of Genetic Psychology*, *162*(1), 41–55.

About the Editor and Contributors

Mari Riojas-Cortez is professor and chair of Early Childhood Studies at California State University–Channel Islands. She received her PhD from the University of Texas at Austin in curriculum and instruction, with a concentration in early childhood education and multilingual studies (bilingual education). Her research focuses on Latino family engagement (in early childhood contexts), young children's play in early childhood dual-language settings, and early childhood teacher education. Dr. Riojas-Cortez has published in major journals including the *International Journal of Early Childhood, Journal of Early Childhood Research, Journal of Early Childhood Teacher Education, Bilingual Research Journal,* and *Young Children,* among others. She is coauthor of the book *Families as Partners in Education: Families and Schools Working Together* (10th edition) and is editor of two accepted books that focus on diversity in early childhood teacher education. Dr. Riojas-Cortez's experience with early childhood settings began in the Harlandale Independent School District in San Antonio, Texas, as a bilingual prekindergarten teacher. She has been an early childhood educator for 30 years and has worked and served in the early childhood field in different capacities. Dr. Riojas-Cortez received the Outstanding Early Childhood Teacher Educator Award in 2019 from the National Association of Early Childhood Teacher Educators, and was selected as Exchange Leader by the Exchange Leadership Initiative sponsored by Childcare Exchange for her contributions to the field of early childhood education, also in 2019. She served as editor for *Dimensions of Early Childhood* for 7 years, and is currently on the editorial board for the *Journal of Early Childhood Teacher Education.*

***

Assumpta Aneas Alvarez is an associate professor in the Department of Research Methodology and Educational Diagnosis at the University of Barcelona since 1998. She is the principal of the consolidated research group GREDI (Research Group in Intercultural Education; www.ub.edu/gredi/). She is a coordinator of the Inclusion, Equity and Well-Being area at the Institute of Research in Education (IRE; www.ub.edu/ire/). Dr. Aneas Alvarez's research interests concern topics such as inclusive education, intercultural and interreligious dialogue, and participatory methods of research.

Kimberly Davidson is an assistant professor in the Department of Human Development and Family Studies at Central Michigan University. She holds a BA in history and an MS in child and family studies, both from the University of Tennessee. She earned her PhD in child and family studies at Syracuse University. She teaches early childhood development courses as well as courses focusing on oppression, diversity, and cultural competence. Dr. Davidson's research interests include early development of racial awareness, racial/ethnic identity development, and cultural continuity between home and early childhood education settings.

Flora Farago is an assistant professor in Human Development and Family Studies at Stephen F. Austin State University (SFA). Flora has a background in developmental psychology and early childhood education. She was born in Budapest, Hungary, and moved to Texas in 1998, where she earned her BA and MS degrees in psychology at the University of Texas at Dallas. She earned a PhD in family and human development from Arizona State University in 2016). Dr. Farago's teaching and research interests center around children's prejudice and stereotype development, antibias curricula, and inclusive early childhood education regarding race and gender. She is particularly interested in the link between research and community activism. She collaborates with colleagues and organizations nationally and internationally, including the Indigo Cultural Center (indigoculturalcenter.org), Local to Global Justice (localtoglobal.org), the Jirani Project (jiraniproject.org/), and the Girl Child Network (girlchildnetwork.org). Dr. Farago has published and presented her work at national and international outlets, and recently coedited a special issue entitled *Confronting and Countering Bias and Oppression through Early Childhood Policy and Practice*.

Montserrat Freixa Niella is an associate professor in the Department of Research Methodology and Educational Diagnosis at the University of Barcelona (Catalonia, Spain). She was vice dean of the Faculty of Education and is now the head of the program of Student Support at this faculty. Dr. Freixa Niella is a researcher in the consolidated research group TRALS (transitions at the university, competencies, tutoring; www.ub.edu/trals/). Her research interests concern topics such as family with disabled children, transitions, interreligious dialogue. mfreixa@ub.edu.

Terry Husband is an associate professor of Early Childhood Literacy at Illinois State University in Normal, Illinois. Dr. Husband teaches courses related to literacy instruction and assessment and student diversity issues in education. His research interests concern anti-racist education in early childhood classrooms and literacy development in Black boys.

Janice Kroeger is currently a professor in Curriculum and Instruction and graduate program coordinator of Early Childhood Education at Kent State University. Dr. Kroeger is best known for scholarship in family-school-community relations focusing on diversity, identity, and inclusion. She has published numerous articles, book chapters, and one recent book related to children, elders, and the earth. Her work focuses on political and social issues and cultural change in early childhood classrooms. Dr. Kroeger is a qualitative researcher using an eclectic blend of conceptual frameworks including critical, discursive, material culture, and feminist-oriented and ethnographic methodologies.

Wilma Robles-Meléndez, is professor of Early Childhood Education and Leadership in the Department of Higher Education, Leadership and Instructional Technology at the Fischler College of Education and School of Criminal Justice of Nova Southeastern University (Fort Lauderdale, Florida). Dr. Robles-Meléndez has over 25 years of experience as an early childhood educator and teacher educator. Her professional experiences also include service as a classroom teacher, school principal, and state early childhood general supervisor. Her research focuses on multicultural and social justice issues with attention on children's immigration issues and culturally responsive practices for children and families. An advocate for children and families, she has several publications on diversity issues and is an active member and presenter at state, national, and international organizations.

Angelina Sánchez Martí is currently a Postdoctoral Fellow at the Department of Systematic and Social Pedagogy at the Autonomous University of Barcelona (UAB). She holds a PhD in education and society from the University of Barcelona. She is an official researcher of the interuniversity and interdisciplinary research center CER-Migracions, focused on the study of international migrations. Dr. Sánchez Martí has been actively involved in research related to intercultural and interreligious dialogue, citizenship education, and values.

Ruth Vilà-Baños is an associate professor in the Department of Research Methodology and Educational Diagnosis at the University of Barcelona since 1999. She is a researcher in the consolidated research group GREDI (Research Group in Intercultural Education; www.ub.edu/gredi/). Dr. Vilà-Baños is a member of the board of directors of Institute of Research in Education (IRE; www.ub.edu/ire/). Her research interests concern topics such as intercultural education, intercultural competences, and intercultural and interreligious dialogue.

Kenya E. Wolff is an assistant professor in Early Childhood Education and the director of the Willie Price Laboratory School at the University of Mississippi. Dr. Wolff's experience as a classroom teacher and administrator allows her to bring real-world knowledge to the students she teaches. These experiences range from public school teacher and toddler teacher in corporate child care, to assistant director of a program for bilingual children, to director of a private preschool/kindergarten. Beyond her work in the classroom, she has served as a board member for the Texas and Florida Association for the Education of Young Children and the Mississippi Early Childhood Association, working at the state level on policy issues that impact the lives of young children and their families. Dr. Wolff's research focuses on whole child development, including work on the benefits of yoga, mindfulness, and antibias curriculum. She currently holds a position on the editorial board for the Southern Early Childhood Association Journal, *Dimensions*, and as an associate editor for the journal, *International Critical Childhood Studies*.

www.ingramcontent.com/pod-product-compliance
Lightning Source LLC
Chambersburg PA
CBHW020753230426
43665CB00009B/576